Troublesome Boy

Harold Rosen

Published by the English and Media Centre 1993
136 Chalton Street London NW1 1RX

Distributed in Britain by NATE 50 Broomfield Road
Sheffield S8 OXJ

© Harold Rosen
All Rights Reserved

Printed by BPCC Wheatons Exeter

ISBN 0 907016 04 9

Acknowledgements

'The Politics of Writing'. This is the text of a paper presented in Detroit in 1983 to the conference of the National Council of Teachers of English. It first appeared in a shortened version in *New Readings: Contributions to an understanding of literacy*, K. Kimberley, M. Meek, J. Miller, eds, A. and C. Black, 1992.

'Talk as Autobiography'. Paper presented to a conference, Talk a Medium for Learning and Change, Peel Board of Education, Toronto, 1991.

'Stories at Work'. This article first appeared in *By Word of Mouth,* Derek Jones and Mary Medlicott, eds, Channel 4 Television, 1989.

'The Autobiographical Impulse'. First published in *Linguistics in Context: Connecting Observation and Understanding*, Deborah Tanner, ed, Ablex, 1988.

Contents

Foreword 4

Collage 5

Autobiography

Comrade Rosie Rosen 11
Troublesome Boy 23
Kleptomania 30
Not Becoming a Lawyer 44
Cribs 54
Not Yet 69
Penmanship 79
Zeider 86
Afterword: Missing Person 87

Stories

Avrum's Overcoat 94
The Tailor Who Couldn't Tell Stories ... 103

Yiddish-English Glossary 110

Articles

The Politics of Writing 113
Talk as Autobiography 131
We Are Our Stories 147
The Autobiographical Impulse .. 152

Foreword

This book begins with a collage of quotations and you could say that the whole book is a collage of pieces I have written at different times and for quite different purposes. Books, like stories, should have strong digestive systems. This one consists of somewhat autobiographical stories, a couple of versions of folk stories and some reflective papers on narrative in general and autobiography in particular. It was Michael Simons, my editor, who suggested that sort of blend and after some timid hesitation I liked it.

The autobiographical stories all turn on memories of my schooling, the events and the people. But I have taken conscious liberties with my memories and, as always, my memory must have taken liberties of which I am unaware. So my mother appears somewhat differently in different stories. She is a kind of composite figure. However, in 'Comrade Rosie Rosen' I have tried to avoid consciously changing or adding to what I remember. What makes me call the stories autobiographical is that I have tried to be faithful to the central truth of my recollections.

The names of my closest friends, fellow students and teachers change from tale to tale. In the papers which follow there are some passages here and there which echo moments in the stories. It's the other way round really. They were written before the stories. In fact, I've selected them from many papers, either buried in journals and in published collections or delivered at conferences and never published.

Some thank-yous are, as ever, due. First and foremost to the Pincer Movement, my wife, Betty, and my son, Michael, who between them propelled me to this enterprise; then to Jane Miller, good friend and colleague, who looked at the stories, egged me on and asked an awkward question (see Afterword); to Michael Simons, already mentioned, an old hand at the kind of midwifery a book like this needs.

Collage

This small compilation was inspired by 'Benjamin's ideal of producing a work consisting entirely of quotations, one that was mounted so masterfully that it could dispense with accompanying texts....'
Hannah Arendt, Introduction to Walter Benjamin's *Illuminations*, Fontana, 1973.

The writer has to gather whatever's there: sometimes too much, sometimes too little, sometimes nothing at all. (p115)
It's easy after all not to be a writer. Most people aren't writers, and very little harm comes to them. (p121)
Julian Barnes, *Flaubert's Parrot*, Picador, 1985.

My main problem is to try and understand what happened to me. My trajectory may be described as miraculous, I suppose - an ascension to a place where I don't belong. And so to be able to live in a world that is not mine I must try to understand both things: what it means to have an academic mind - how such is created - and at the same time what was lost in acquiring it. For that reason, even if my work - my full work - is a sort of autobiography, it is a work for people who have the same sort of trajectory and the same need to understand.
Pierre Bourdieu in conversation with Terry Eagleton at the Institute of Contemporary Arts, 15 May, 1991.

Man is always a storyteller! He lives surrounded by his and others' myths. With them he sees everything in his life, no matter what befalls him and he seeks to live his life as though he were telling it.
Jean Paul Sartre, cited by Gergen K.J. and Gergen M.M. in Sarbin and Scheibe, *Social Identity* Praeger, 1983.

Yes, every dead person leaves a little gift, his or her memory, and demands that we take care of it. We must supply friends for those who have none. So law, justice, is more reliable than all our forgetful tendernesses, than our tears, so speedily dried. This magistracy is History. And the dead are, to speak in the manner of Roman law, those wretched people with whom a magistrate must be concerned. Never in my career have I lost sight of this task of the historian. I have given to many of the very forgotten dead that assistance which I myself will have need of. I have exhumed them for a second life. They now live amongst those of us who feel ourselves to be their parents, their friends. Thus a family is made, a city shared by the living and the dead.

J. Michelet, *Oevres Completes* XX1 p268 (cited by Anderson, see below).

All profound changes of consciousness, by their very nature, bring with them their characteristic amnesias. Out of such oblivions, in specific historical circumstances, spring narratives. After experiencing the physiological and emotional changes produced by puberty it's impossible to 'remember' the consciousness of childhood. How many thousands of days passsed between infancy and early adulthood vanish beyond direct recall! How strange it is to need another's help to learn that this naked baby in the yellowed photograph, sprawled happily on rug or cot, is you. The photograph, fine child of the age of mechanical production, is only the most peremptory of a huge modern accumulation of documentary evidence (birth certificates, diaries, report cards, letters, medical records and the like) which simultaneously records a certain apparent continuity and emphasises its loss from memory. Out of this estrangement comes a conception of personhood, identity (yes, you and that naked baby are identical) which, because it cannot be 'remembered', must be narrated.

Benedict Anderson, *Imagined Communities* Verso, 1983.

To narrate means to speak here and now with an authority that derives from having been (literally and metaphorically) there and then.

Carlo Ginsberg, *Ecstasies: Deciphering the Witches' Sabbath* Penguin Books, 1991.

The subject replays his identity, or rather his identities, by ceaseless and never finished stories. Through the story he ties together the fragile threads which allow him to be himself just a little. The story allows the subject at every moment to actualize an image - perhaps not coherent but at least tending towards coherence - of what he was through what he did, an image he

identifies with and upon which he rests to conquer his future.
Jacques Brés, 'De la production d'identité dans la mise en récit d'une action carnavalesque' *Langage et Societé,* No 62, decembre, 1992.

....it is better to tell stories than remain silent even though there is no definitive and best story .... no last story that, once told, would leave all future storytellers without employment.
Michael Walzer, *Interpretation and Social Criticism,* Harvard Univ Press, 1987.

I once dreamt I was telling stories and felt someone patting my foot in encouragement. I looked down and saw that I was standing on the shoulders of an old woman who was steadying my ankles and smiling up at me.

I said to her, 'No, no, come stand on my shoulders, for you are old and I am young.'

'No, no,' she insisted, 'this is the way it is supposed to be.'

I saw that she stood on the shoulders of a woman far older than she, who stood on the shoulders of a woman even older, who stood on the shoulders of a woman in robes, who stood on the shoulders of another soul, who stood on the shoulders ....

I believed the old dream-woman about the way it was supposed to be. The nurture for telling stories comes from those who have gone before. Telling or hearing stories draws its power from a towering column of humanity joined to one another across time and space, elaborately dressed in the rags and robes or nakedness of their time ....
Clarissa Pinkola Estes, *Women who Run with Wolves,* Rider, 1992.

Memories are our most enduring characteristic. In old age we can remember our childhood eighty or more years ago; a chance remark can conjure up a face, a name, a vision of sea or mountains, once seen and apparently long forgotten. Memory defines who we are and shapes the way we act more closely than any other single act of of personhood. All of life is a trajectory from experienced past to unknown future, illuminated only during the always receding instant we call the present, the moment of our actual conscious experience. Yet our present appears continuous with our past, grows out of it, is shaped by it, because of our capacity for memory. It is this which prevents

the past from being lost, as unknowable as the future. It is memory which thus provides time with its arrow.
Steven Rose, *The Making of Memory*, Bantam Press, 1992.

When one looks to the social practices by which social life is accomplished, one finds - with surprising frequency - people telling stories to one another, as a means of giving cognitive and emotional coherence to experience, constructing and negotiating social identity.
Richard Bauman, *Story, Performance and Event*, Cambridge Univ Press, 1986.

....involuntary memory, one in which the materials of memory no longer appear singly, as images, but tell us about a whole, amorphously and formlessly, indefinitely and weightily, in the same way as the weight of his net tells the fisherman about his catch.
Walter Benjamin, *Illuminations*, Fontana, 1973.

Just as every family quickly acquires a history, and just as its memory becomes enriched from day to day, since the family's recollections become more precise and fixed in their personal form, the family progressively tends to interpret in its own manner the conceptions it borrows from society.
Maurice Halbwachs, *On Collective Memory*, Univ of Chicago Press, 1992.

The social meaning of memory, like its internal structure and its mode of transmission, is little affected by its truth; all that matters is that it be believed at least at some level - for one shouldn't forget folk tales, which are commemorations of the past as well, even though they are not told as strictly believable.
J. Fentress and C. Wickham, *Social Memory*, Blackwell, 1992.

Yet just as human beings make their own history, they also make their cultures and ethnic identities. No one can deny the persisting continuities of long traditions, sustained habitations, national languages, and cultural geographies but there seems no reason except fear and prejudice to keep insisting on their separation and distinctiveness, as if that was all human life was about.
....all cultures are involved in one another; none is single

and pure, all are hybrid, heterogeneous, extraordinarily differentiated, and unmonolithic.
Edward Said, *Culture and Imperialism* Chatto and Windus, 1993.

They [life stories HR] should be seen, not as blurred experience, as disorderly masses of fragments, but as shaped accounts in which some incidents were dramatized, others contextualised, yet others passed over in silence through a process of narrative shaping in which both conscious and unconscious, myth and reality, played significant parts.
R. Samuel and P. Thompson, *The Myths We Live By*, Routledge, 1990.

I have only one faithful guide on which I can rely, that is the chain of feelings which have marked the development of my being, and by means of them, that of the events that were their causes and effects. I may make factual omisions, transpositions, mistakes about dates, but I cannot go wrong about what I have felt, not about what my feelings have led me to do, and that is what it is all about.
J-J. Rousseau, *The Confessions*, 1781, trans. 1953, Penguin Books.

I persist in thinking that autobiography is an extension of fiction, rather than the reverse, that the shape of life comes first from imagination rather than experience.
Jerome Bruner, *The Autobiographical Process*, n.d. unpublished

....ordinary language is extraordinary because at its heart it is precisely that realm of values, intentions and purposes which is often assumed to be the exclusive property of literature.
Stanley Fish, *Is there a Text in this Class?*, Harvard Univ Press, 1980.

....each new social movement needs to begin with the hard work of creating its own collective memories. Socialism has struggled to recreate the submerged memories of working class people, black movements have rediscovered their roots, feminists the suppressed history of women. These collective memories, whether imposed from above as ruling ideologies or forged from below by the struggle of emerging social movements, are the means whereby we remember the past, our history, and therefore they both guide our present actions and shape our futures. nothing in biology in general, or in our human life in particular, makes sense except in the context of memory, of history.

Steven Rose, *Making of Memory* Bantam Press 1992.

In a Hasidic village, so the story goes, Jews were sitting together in a shabby inn one Sabbath evening. They were all local people with the exception of one person no one knew, a very poor, ragged man who was squatting in a dark corner at the back of the room. All sorts of things were discussed, and then it was suggested that everyone should tell what wish he would make if one were granted him. One man wanted money; another wished for a son-in-law; a third dreamed of a new carpenter's bench; and so everyone spoke in turn. After they had finished, only the beggar in the dark corner was left. Reluctantly and hesitantly he answered the question. 'I wish I were a powerful king reigning over a big country. Then, some night while I was asleep in my palace, an enemy would invade my country, and by dawn his horsemen would penetrate to my castle and meet with no resistance. Roused from my sleep, I wouldn't even have time to dress and I would have to flee in my shirt. Rushing over hill and dale and through forests day and night, I would finally arrive safely here at the bench in this corner. This is my wish.' The others exchanged uncomprehending glances. 'And what good would this have done you?' someone asked. 'I'd have a shirt,' was the answer.

Walter Benjamin, *Illuminations*, Fontana, 1973.

Comrade Rosie Rosen

I was eleven, sitting on a hard chair, looking at the man across the desk. He looked weary, perhaps even cross. My mother was sitting on a chair next to me. She too was looking across the desk at the man. I thought I could detect the glint of battle in her eye, but the man hadn't noticed. He wasn't looking at either of us but down at the buff-coloured folder which he frowned at while he was opening it.

We had ended up in this room after crossing Westminster Bridge. From the north side you gaze across the river at County Hall. I had seen it from there several times - a very important building, very governmental, solid, expensive, closed. I had never wondered what went on in it. I don't think I knew that they governed London from there and I certainly didn't know that somewhere in there they governed my education. As we crossed the bridge County Hall expanded, spreading its long facade right along the South Bank of the river. There seemed to be no way into its white coldness. How did anybody get in? Was there a special side door for nobodies? This was not going to be easy. But my mother was not touched by doubt. I could tell by her walk and the hold of her head. She led me round to the back without hesitation. Had she been here before? We went up wide steps into a high entrance hall. Uniformed men asked her business and one gave her directions like a policeman. We trekked up wide staircases into a labyrinth of expensive wood, along panelled corridors, our shoes clacking on polished parquet. We were, I felt sure, in enemy territory. County Hall men and women passed us about their business, intent, silent. I found them sinister.

My mother found the room we wanted. Its ordinariness came as a surprise - drab walls, well-worn lino, a few stacks of files on the floor, books and pamphlets leaning crazily on a set of shelves. A tray of papers on the desk was overspilling a little. I would have liked to be away from there, back on my side of the river, walking freely along the Embankment, taking in boats, bridges, public gardens and saunterers.

The man across the desk looked up and gazed at my mother without saying a word. Teachers do that, I thought. It's how they get on top of you from the word go. My mother wore for the occasion her best black gloves, a newish grey hat and a fox fur. Gloves, hat, fur - she was putting on the style. The man began talking in a rusty voice, affecting infinite patience and civility, cultivated in dealing with the lower orders, especially those from the East End. I heard heavy condescension and controlled insolence. I worried desperately. My scholarship to the grammar school was at stake.

- Before I hear what you have to say, Mrs Rosen, and I shall do, rest assured, you simply must understand I have noted all the details. I have read your letter most carefully. I see from the form you've filled out that you and your husband became U.S. citizens in 1913. I am very sorry to tell you that makes the boy an alien. You won't have read the regulations, of course. Oh, so sorry, you have? Well, they are very clear, aren't they? We are obliged to see that all conditions are met before we can ....

- Just a minute, just a minute. No one has asked me about what happened to my citizenship after I came back to England in 1922. You certainly haven't, have you? I reclaimed my British citizenship in 1924 after they changed the law. There's quite a few things which concern this scholarship which I've not been asked about.

- Mrs Rosen, we have checked the details very thoroughly.

- You haven't got all the details so how can you have checked them?

At this point she took out of her bag a little sheaf of papers. I marvelled at her composure. The desk-man made an attempt to speak but my mother, certain she had the initiative, cut him off.

- No, no. Don't rush me. Are you in a hurry? Let's go through these papers one by one. And you should know that my local councillor, Mr Silver, will be coming to see you and my MP, Mr John Scurr, tells me he'll be writing to you.

The official's manner was changing. Not that he became affable, but he was no longer dismissive and patronising. I had by now shed all my discomfort and sat revelling in my mother's aplomb. I was sure I'd get that scholarship.

I had heard my mother confronting officialdom before - across desks and counters and on our own doorstep. I loved the ways in which she could hold her own with the best of them, just as I winced when I heard nervous old folk struggling for English words to cope with men and their pens and papers and well-timed ways of looking over the tops of their glasses. I admit fully that I thought my mother was something special for all sorts of reasons, some of which don't look very good now. Yes, I know too that mothers are special to their children who are loved by them, defended by them and who are always there. But that's not what I mean at all. I was, I suppose, what I can only call a mother snob, inflated ridiculously by all the ways in which she was different from the Jewish mums who surrounded me. First of all she was born in England, right there in Stepney, not in Minsk, Vilna or Odessa. It followed that she'd been to school in England and after getting a job as a cashier in a large grocer's shop in Aldgate she took extra classes at the People's Palace so she spoke Real English. In the family it sounded Jewish. After all, you can't speak of Passover, a barmitzvah, how to make cheese blintzes without throwing in a few Yiddish and Hebrew words and phrases and even direct translations from Yiddish. But my mother could drop all that very easily and posh up her English when the occasion demanded it. When she sometimes overdid it and made her lips look different my pride went sour on me. Usually I took great pleasure in her sounding so English, believing that it was mostly this which gave her the confidence to cross the frontiers of the ghetto to go to theatres and meetings and to take us on trips into the country. I was pleased she didn't speak to me in Yiddish and I indecently discarded it totally as soon as I could. To me her English made her a cut above, several cuts.

At eight I knew she was the cleverest woman in the world. If not in the world then at least between Gardiner's Corner and Burdett Road. I knew, too, that she'd read millions of books - Whitechapel Library was one of her haunts. She had quite a few old books on the shelves of a small battered bookcase in her bedroom, bought, I suppose, for pence from market stalls or in fundraising bazaars. Once I could read I used to puzzle over the titles. So many of them seemed perversely opaque - *Hypatia, Quo Vadis, Pygmalion, Erewhon, Anti-Duhring, The Ragged Trousered Philanthropists* and *King of the Schnorrers*. I had gradually come to the conclusion that she knew every word in the English language. I used to sit on the floor and read when she was in bed in the morning. Once I was struggling through *Robinson Crusoe* because someone had given it to me as a birthday present and because it was brand new with a brilliant red cover, in the middle of which was pasted a picture of Robinson himself bare foot and thatched all over. But inside the print was too small, the black and white illustrations murky and the language elusive. The compensation was that if there was a word I couldn't understand I'd ask my encyclopaedic mother.

- Mum, what's an ague? (I pronounced it to rhyme with plague.)
- A what? Something wrong there. Read the sentence out to me.
- 'I was stricken with an ague'.
- Ah, I see, you should say ay-gue. It means a fever.

I was seven. I was sitting for the umpteenth time in a large seedy room in Cable Street. A crowd of men and women were sitting on an assortment of battered old chairs under a blue-grey swirl of reeking cigarette and pipe smoke. Against one flaking wall was propped the red banner with a yellow hammer and sickle in the middle of it. Down one end Milly was making lemon tea on an old black stove and serving portions of cheese cake. I was reading *Film Fun* and getting impatient for my mother to get me some of that cheese cake. These were The Comrades at a meeting of The Party in what were always called The Premises. That evening we'd struggled through the damp of Cable Street, across the puddles of the smelly yard and joined The Comrades. I knew in a half-truculent way that there was not going to be much in this for me. From time to time I looked up from my comic and tried to listen to the very serious men and women. Not easy. Each speaker took a long time and there was very little I could understand. Out there, nobody else talked like this, pointing didactic fingers and punching the air. I knew some of them very well for they often came to the house to deliver 'literature' (I had trouble with that word for a long time). When they did, they talked like everyone else - mostly. A few of them gave me their time and joked and told me stories and one of them sang Yiddish songs. Tobias, whom I had heard speaking like an avenging angel, gave me a copy of William Morris's *News from Nowhere* and wrote in it, 'The fault, dear Brutus, lies not in our stars but in ourselves that we are underlings'. I couldn't make much of that at the time. Keep it till later, he had said. One day he arrived with a cardboard box full of volumes of an out-of-date encyclopaedia - I think it was Harmsworth's. Volume Seven was missing but we sat together looking at the pictures and he kept up an instructive patter.

- You'll see. Some day this will help you with your studies. It's all in here.

They were shoved higgledy-piggledy in the cupboard on the landing outside my bedroom and I often pulled out a volume and turned the pages. I liked Tobias, even when he was orating at The Premises.

This evening as usual the argot which so bewitched them was rolling out. They spoke of the dictatorship of the proletariat, surplus value, the balance of class forces, the crimes of the bourgeoisie. There were dark denunciations of class traitors and deviationists. My mother could speak this language, too. She was at a table at the front of the meeting as Branch Secretary with four other Comrades. After the meeting, long after I had finished my cheesecake and some lemonade, she stayed behind to plan leafleting, a poster parade, canvassing - activities which I'd sometimes be drawn into and be given a placard to hold or a tin to shake. Before The Comrades left The Premises they stopped to take some pamphlets from the piles on the trestle table. My mother took some too. They were as baffling to me as the speeches. They were called things like 'The Final Crisis of Capitalism', 'The Ninth Plenum of the Comintern', 'The Soviet Path to Peace'. I used to look for the ones with pictures in. There were always pictures of men in jail - The Twelve Class War Prisoners (in England), The Meerut Prisoners (in India), Tom Mooney (in the U.S.), marchers with slogan banners, strikers outside their factories and confrontations with police. They became the dominant icons of my childhood and my mother was in the thick of all this. Look at her speaking and them listening. What a woman!

My friends' mothers were not like that, loveable though I found them, plumply installed in their kitchens with their magic recipes, overflowing with affection. They were always good to me, stroked my hair and found me noshy tit-bits. They clearly thought life must be hard for a little boy whose mother was always schlepping him to meetings. All the same, if there was trouble with a landlord they were round to our house like a shot.

I was eight and it was May Day, Tuesday morning. My sister and I were standing in a municipal dust-cart. It was a brand new one, gleaming buff paint and the splendour of Stepney's coat of arms on the side. The grand cart-horses were perfectly groomed and their brasses were gleaming. For this day they were decked out with red and yellow ribbons plaited into their manes and tails. Large rosettes bloomed by their ears. There were thirty or so other little children in the cart with us. I looked over the side at the horses' huge bums and twitching ears. How did they know that they must stand still? Why didn't they lumber off down the road? When would the driver come? I couldn't wait. I had a little ache of anxiety about how we were going to find my mother in the milling thousands in Hyde Park. 'Silly', said my sister. 'Don't you remember last year? We always find her. She comes to get us.' So we concentrated on cheering the contingents, passing us with their banners, placards and bands. A fairground was flowing along the street. We were in the dustcart because we were too small to march all the way and our Labour council, like others, had provided their new carts for the kids and perhaps to add a brave dash of fresh paint for the parade. This was not yet another bitter taking to the streets calling for the release of somebody or hands off something or the end of cuts. This was a street festival, a non-stop party. I was just old enough to know that the tradition then was that you took the May Day holiday, no matter what day it fell on. Workers for Labour Councils were given the day off. I knew too that this was a school day and that we were absentees, a cartload of us. My sister and I started getting at our wurst sandwiches and someone was handing out bottles of pop. The cart moved off and we wore our arms out waving at the folk lining the Whitechapel Road. We sang that we were going to hang somebody or other (Joynson-Hicks, was it?) on the sour apple tree when the revolution comes and hurrah for the

Bolshie Boys who didn't care a little bit. Then we entered the hostile silence of the City where gents stood staring stonily. Occasionally one of them raged and shook an umbrella like a man in a cartoon. Safe in our cart we laughed and booed and laughed and jumped up and down.

I knew all about May Day. How could I not know? My mother had instructed me over the years.

- They've got their days, plenty of them. Alexandra Day, Armistice Day, Empire Day. And we've got our day, just one, but it's ours. All theirs are for wars, for charity, for showing off with soldiers. They've stuck up their monuments all over the place. Generals and conquerors with soldiers dying like flies all round them and lists of all those poor young men, nebbich, killed in their wars. And they always trot out a priest or parson or rabbi to show how holy it all is. We've got our day, our festival, the workers' holiday. It's all ours and nothing to do with them.

She could go on like this for a long time till it became an incantation. In a sort of trance I knew she had to be right. The trouble was I was dazzled by the Lord Mayor's Show and its tableaux and that golden coach. As for soldiers, I wouldn't ever have dared to admit to her that I tingled when they marched by with their shining bands. and I didn't know who 'they' were who set up all those days. All the same, May Day in the cart was best, I was sure of that.

The next day I took an absence note to school, nothing very elaborate. 'My son, Harold, was absent from school yesterday because it was May Day, the workers' holiday.' Not a word was said about it and I knew why. The first time my mother had kept me away on a May Day my teacher had grilled me about it. Where had I been? I couldn't bring myself to tell the truth so I became shifty and mumbled nonsense. She lost patience with me and sent me to the Head. It didn't take him long to extract from me that I had been on the May Day demonstration. His eyes bulged and he poked me in the shoulder. He was shouting very close to my face. What could my mother be thinking of? Did I realise that she could be taken to court? Did she think she could keep me away whenever it took her fancy?

As soon as I got home I spilled it all out, especially the poking in the shoulder and being taken to court.

- Court? We'll see about that. And I can tell you he'd better keep his hands off you.

The next day she was up at the school. I wanted to hear

every word of what had happened.

- I don't think we'll have any more mishegas about May Day again.
- What did he say? What did he say? What about going to court?
- Court! Don't make me laugh. It wasn't mentioned.

My guess was that Mr Margolis got an earful of Them and Their Days and Us and Our Days. According to her, it all ended up very amicably and by the end she was taking coffee with him like a distinguished visitor. I heard her telling my zeider about it amidst laughter.

- We had a nice long talk. Mind you, he nearly took the wind out of my sails. So polite, butter wouldn't melt in his mouth. He says, 'Mrs Rosen, I think there has been a little misunderstanding'. So I think to myself, I know how to manage this. Mustn't push the little man too hard. Best to give a bit of ground for starters. So I say, 'Well, you know, Mr Margolis, maybe I should have dropped you a line beforehand but I thought to myself, a man like you was bound to know it was May Day and, how shall I say, put two and two together.' 'Mrs Rosen,' he says, 'I don't mind saying this to you. I can tell you what it's really about. Truancy in this area is a problem. You've got to watch it like a hawk - helping in the shop, minding the baby, went to my auntie's - you can guess the sort of thing.' Then I tell him why May Day is a different matter altogether. 'Of course,' he says, 'of course.' And this you won't believe, he ends up with, 'Well, we're all socialists nowadays, Mrs Rosen.' My grandfather slapped his leg, pushed back his glasses and roared. I wondered why they found that so funny. It became part of the family lore, though, and was cited when anyone mentioned Mr Margolis. I knew now I'd have no trouble on future May Days. On this occasion my mother's brief note was meant as a tactful reminder of the negotiations over the coffee cups. As I got older I began to be troubled by the fact that as far as I could tell I was the only one in the school who stayed away. What were the other parents doing about Our Day? You could say that I'm still asking that question.

I was eight still and making my way to school filled with a sick fatalism. There was misery ahead and nothing I could do would stave it off. I was going to Empire Day which the school turned into an all-day jamboree with prayers, hymns, dancing, playlets, readings and above all the grand parade in the playground at the start of the day, to get us in the right frame of mind. We all stomped round in our idea of military marching, a strange little parody, swinging arms, knees up high and feet thumping hard on the asphalt, heads rigid. Small boys and girls in the newest clothes their parents could manage paraded in front of the dull red barrack which towered over them. The five-year-olds, somewhat bemused, got out of step, tripped over each other, and revelled in every second. The tedium and dangers of a routine school day had been declared null and void. All the joy was spiced with competition. Every child brought a Union Jack as they'd been told to do. For days the flags had been on sale in every little sweetshop where they flowered in little tubs next to the front door. If you were really poor you had to be satisfied with a ha'penny one, a pathetic rectangle of thin card glued to a stick with the thickness of a knitting needle. It wasn't going to stand up to a day's waving and jousting but while it was brightly new it could join the colour of the carnival in the morning sunshine. There it would have to stand comparison with those brought by youngsters whose parents could do much better. They arrived with real bunting ones which fluttered properly. There were a few which were taller that the children who held them with golden spikes on top like Prussian helmets. Ostentatious declarations of loyalty, they belonged with the prayers for the Royal Family on the synagogue walls.

On this fine summer's morning I turned grumpily into Myrdle Street, passing the other children flaunting their finery and flags at each other. Not me. I was in my usual old jersey and scuffed shoes and no flag. My mother was not going to have me tainted with the iniquity of Empire and at least one person was going to crack the enameled surface of unanimity - me. Carefully she had lectured me about what she thought Empire really meant. She had lots of pamphlets on the subject with appalling pictures in them of floggings, shootings and hangings presided over by men in pith helmets. They haunt me to this post-holocaust day. As ever, I only partly understood what she was saying but I approved of all of it. It was my mother saying all this and she knew. She knew the truth about Empire as she knew about everything else, schooled as she was by those Cable Street conclaves. Which was all very well but she had made quite clear that there was going to be no flag for me and no poshing up. It was one thing to be dazzled by her inside knowledge but quite another to be selected as the representative of her principles, defying the British Empire all by myself.

I'd had a taste of this before. Young as I was, I had learned to grit my teeth and stay seated next to my mother in the cinema when, at the end of the show, they played the National Anthem and a picture of King George V was flashed on the screen. All around me seats banged, people jumped up and stiffened their backs. I studied my feet. As they left they glowered and swore at us and sometimes jostled us a bit. I was frightened certainly of being hurt, but the real pain was the sense of isolation and difference. Only my mother, facing them all without a flicker of doubt, stopped me from rushing out in tears.

The martyrdom of Empire Day was going to be quite another thing. I was going to have to bear it all on my own, in broad daylight, amongst my friends, in front of all the teachers, for a long, long day. The anonymous rigid backs in the cinema were nowhere near as fearsome as the prospect of angry, shocked faces in the school yard. I was a small boy approaching the school gate, wanting to turn tail before retribution overtook me. I caught sight of Solly waving a big flag. His father owned an embroidery shop. Lily Kravitz, in a blue velvet dress with a big bow at the back, came running towards me, all friendly as usual.

- My mum says they're going to give us all sweets and an apple each.

Then she took a close look at me, my flaglessness, my old jersey and my sulky face and ran off to her friends. And there was Monty whose father was always talking to my zeider about the affairs of the Tailors and Garment Workers' Union. He had his shabbas clothes on all right and he had a flag.

I sneaked into my classroom. My teacher at the time was Miss Waters who was a leg smacker and finger poker. I hadn't been in the room more than a minute or two when I felt her eyeing me strangely. She knew nothing of my mother's little chat with the Head on the subject of May Day. I huddled in my desk amidst the excited children but I couldn't hide from Miss Waters. She made her way towards me and asked me to come to the front of the class. I steeled myself. She whispered in my ear in an unfamiliar, kind voice.

- Harold, didn't you have a ha'penny to buy a flag?

She had taken one look at my clothes and my misery face and assumed I was too poor to buy even the cheapest flag.

- Here's a ha'penny, she said. The late bell hasn't gone yet. Nip over the road and buy yourself a flag. For goodness' sake look sharp or we'll be starting without you.

It was a warm, understanding, untypical thing for her to do. That made it harder for me. If I had been given a dressing down or threatened or made to stand in the corner, I might have dug out of myself a little bravado, though I doubt it. I was far too demoralised by now. That sympathetic voice was irresistible. The severe Miss Waters, I felt, understood all my trials and my self-pitying torment. I looked up at her, ready to commit a monstrous betrayal. There was my principled mother quite deliberately sending me to school so that I could make my stand and begin my apprenticeship. And here was I on the brink of betraying her, actually rejoicing at having this hump of anxiety taken off my back. I took Miss Waters ha'penny. She was gently pushing me out of the classroom.

- Hurry, she said. We'll be waiting for you.

I was away, out of the gates, down the street, across the road and into the sweetshop with its last few ha'penny flags. Mrs Abrams was baffled at my popping up like this. She gave me an old-fashioned look and sold me a flag. I was back at the school and into the classroom like a flash. I imagined the whole class was relieved that I was back in the fold and they no longer had to be sorry for me and Miss Waters smiled at me. She was soon marshalling us out of the building and into the playground. There we were lined up and we peeled off class by class into the march. Someone had managed to get a piano into the playground and Mr Margolis standing at the keyboard thumped out a military tune. He was surrounded by the staff who looked happy and approving. As we passed the piano party we waved our flags as we'd been told. Three times round, no less, we went. The relief I had felt soon seeped out of me. And by the time I had done my third renegade waving of that flag I was more downcast than I had been, struggling to do without one. Disconsolate when we finally came to a halt, I did not join in singing 'Land of Hope and Glory', as though I could buy my way back to a clear conscience with this gesture.

I suffered the rest of the day's endless festivities. From time to time Miss Waters took a long look at me, perhaps wondering why her ha'penny hadn't done as much for me as she had hoped. I ate my sweets and apple at playtime, though. I walked home slowly, still holding the accursed flag. I pulled it from its stick and tore it into little pieces and pushed them down a grating in Commercial Road. Then I broke up the stick too, and dropped it into a basement in New Road. I sneaked into our house, trying to avoid my mother - not an easy thing to do at the best of times. Soon enough we were in the kitchen together. She scrutinized me with a quick look and said,

- What's the matter, son? It was a bit hard, eh?

She knew what she had let me in for and her voice told me she had had her qualms.

- It sometimes costs to stick up for what you believe in but it's the only way. All the same it was hard for you, wasn't it? I can tell. All day without a flag. That hurt a bit, didn't it?

Then I did the worst thing possible, the very worst thing.

- Yes, I said, it did.

Troublesome Boy

Of course, she thought of it. It wouldn't have crossed my mind.

- It would be nice, she said, a nice thing to do.

- Course, said my sister, you shouldn't get too big for your boots.

- You don't remember, said my mother. Why should you remember? I remember.

- What'll I say to him? 'Remember me? The corner near the window. Your favourite pupil. Turns out I'm a genius. My mother thinks you ought to know. How's the little school going? Punishment book filling up nicely?'

- Such a clever-dick don't need a rehearsal, said my sister.

- Do me a favour, said my mother. You have to have a bit of consideration. You knock your kishkas out for twenty years for a bunch of snotty-nosed momzeirim and in the finish what you got to show for it? Pressers, cutters, button-hole makers, market boys. Why shouldn't he know now and then that one of them won his Matric?

- Passed, I said, together with thirty other future Nobel prize-winners. Passed. You don't win anything. They give you a nice piece of paper you can nail to the wall.

- Pish, pish, said my sister. Pish, pish. Two a penny. It's a nothing.

- He'll go. He'll go, said my mother. A thankyou costs nothing, and you got plenty to thank him for.

- Did I say I wouldn't go?

My mother brushed the crumbs off the table into the palm of her hand and stood looking at them. She was so full of pride she didn't know where to put it all.

So next day I was off to see Mr Margolis, the Headteacher of the elementary school I'd attended until I was eleven. After five years Mr Margolis had not faded. I had forgotten nothing about him and even now decades and decades later he is more vivid than all my other teachers who are now just fuzzy masks. I don't think there are teachers like that any more, mostly because, thank God, they don't want to be like that and in any case the kids won't let them. Margolis was a monster. A single stony glance from him could set your heart quaking. What am I saying? A glance? Just being there was enough. That silent figure in a classroom doorway could freeze the marrows of forty or more case-hardened little hooligans just by being there. That awesome man could beam his terror across the full width of the Whitechapel Road or from the far end of the playground. If I saw that black trilby a hundred yards away I'd seek out a shop doorway or alleyway to press myself into rather than face the ordeal of simply saying, 'Good morning, sir' and raising my cap (a little ritual drilled to a nicety when you went into the Big Boys at seven). He dressed the part, too. No one I knew wore a black jacket and waistcoat, striped trousers, wing collar and spats. Spats, yes, spats. I used to stare at them, hypnotised, under the iron bar of the oak desk. Little felt-like, ankle high gaiters with an elastic strap which went under his shoe. I wondered what they were for. My mother said it was to keep his feet warm. Though I believed she knew everything, right down to the functions of men's clothing, I felt they were some kind of badge of office. He was the Head and no other teacher wore them. The others wore peat-coloured Harris tweeds, all hairy and pouchy, except for Mr Solomons who wore an immaculate double-breasted blazer and dark grey, pure wool flannels with sharp creases. Very smart, yes, but not what you would call headmasterly. And another thing, the pince-nez. The last exquisite refinement of terror, they enlarged his grey eyes, still and unblinking, to a predatory, basilisk, scrutinizing goggle. He haunted my dreams, stalking across vast halls, swishing his cane to winkle me out from a hidey-hole in the cloakroom, contrite and guilty, not of any identifiable crime but of having committed the sin of being. He may have had a wife, and children even. Somewhere, sometime, his face must have thawed into a smile and his voice must have melted into laughter. My fluttering mind could not entertain such an outlandish fiction. Immaculate, he inhabited the brown chipped-tile world of Myrdle Street Elementary School, ruled over it and at nights, roosted immobile in a gruesome eyrie, eyes open, probing the darkness for cowering sinners and backsliders.

In those days, the Head sat at one end of the hall, up on a dais, his desk covered in green baize, backed by the Union Jack and portraits of the King and Queen. It seems to me now that he never left that chair behind the desk from which he could hear and see everything. No chance of his not knowing you were late or had managed to persuade a teacher to let you go to the toilet before playtime. Always you had to run the gauntlet of the Gorgon in the chair. On his desk were the cane, the Punishment Book and a large brass handbell. The cane saw regular service and he had a reserve supply pickling in brine in an aquarium under the window. We tried not to look at it during assemblies. All of us would have admitted to anything, served any penance, had he so much as ruffled his brow with a frown. I suppose it was because we would not have paid the price and the bite of pain would not have delivered its moral message. And the Punishment Book would not have recorded your sins for posterity. Turn to any page and you'd have discovered the Moral Order of Myrdle Street School - the crime, the punishment, the executioner's signature:

Disobedience	4 strokes
Lateness	2 strokes
Impertinence	4 strokes
Damage to school property	6 strokes
Talking in class	2 strokes
Foul Language	6 strokes
Obscene Behaviour	6 strokes

It was Obscene Behaviour when Kossoff pissed over the toilet wall.

I still marvel in a dazed sort of way at how much he could achieve through pure, unsullied fear. He taught us for music lessons and we were assembled in rows in front of the piano in the hall. Someone once told me he was a fine musician and he did teach us some good songs. But at that time I had only one musical ambition. I was ten but there were older boys in Standard Seven, some, of course, with breaking voices. Mr

Margolis would prowl up and down the rows once he had launched us into 'From the Cotswolds and the Chilterns' (where, for God's sake, were they?) or 'Charlie is my Darling' (Charlie? Could that be right?). Up and down the rows he went, his back bent and his ear cocked, all in the holy cause of hunting down what he called grunters. It was a personal crusade from which he never relaxed. 'Please God', I used to pray to myself, 'let me not be a grunter. Let me get all my sums wrong, have too many blotty scratchings-out in my compositions, be caught sniggering and whispering, or even trying and failing to piss over the toilet wall.' Yes, even that, rather than being singled out by Mr Margolis, hand-picked inches from his pince-nez and spats and damned as an incurable grunter. Why? In heaven's name, why? All that happened to grunters was that they were sent to the back of the hall where, provided they did not bat an eyelid, they could indulge themselves to their heart's content, listening to the non-grunters' palpitating voices doing 'Nymphs and Shepherds, Come Away'. It was enough for Mr Margolis to indicate that a grunter was a despicable worm and deservedly an outcast for me to dread ending up on the pariahs' bench at the back of the hall. In the army during rifle inspection when the officer of the day fetched up in front of me, about to give my Lee-Enfield the once-over, I caught a whiff of that same kind of dread. But only a whiff.

It was this same terrifying man who pulled about eight or nine of us out of class to prepare us for the scholarship. A couple of boys a year passed and went on to grammar schools. It was a heavy price to pay to have to sit with Mr Margolis and make our mistakes under his very nose. We were supposed to think it a dazzling privilege to be selected and groomed for stardom. My mother, for instance, couldn't contain her delight.

- The Headmaster teaching you. Personally. Better than that shikke, O'Carroll.

Mr O'Carroll was in her bad books because it was known that he went to a pub at midday where he probably had a modest pint and a sandwich, so that he became in her eyes that gentile reprobate, a shikke, a drunk. He certainly smelled of beer in the afternoons and we used to sing in the playground to the tune of 'Hey Ho Come to the Fair':

Where there's a barrel
There's Jimmy O'Carroll
So hey ho come to the pub.

In fact we quite liked him. But for my mother, the austere and awesome Mr Margolis seemed a much more suitable tutor. I don't know whether he was or wasn't. Perhaps she was very impressed when I told her of one surprising ploy of his. He would give us Latin words and have us try to think up English words derived from them. He'd write up 'scribere, scriptum' and if we were lucky we'd make a list of scribe, inscribe, describe, subscribe, script, scripture. Someone suggested scribble and he didn't seem quite sure. When it came to the exam there was none of this in it at all. Perhaps my mother hadn't got it right but I passed and that vindicated her completely.

- Without him, she said, you'd be sitting in Standard Seven for another three years like those other wooden heads.

So I left for the Grammar School and glory and five years later passed the Matriculation exams. To be honest, I didn't think to myself on hearing my results read out, good old Margolis. If it weren't for him, etc, etc. In fact at that particular joyous moment I didn't think about him at all. It was only when my mother started nagging me to go and see him that Mr Margolis came to mind. The truth is I wasn't keen because I just couldn't see us exchanging pleasantries and having a friendly laugh about the good old days and him telling me he knew all along what a brilliant scholar I was and would I remember him to my mother. I knew it wasn't going to be like that but I also couldn't imagine what it would be like. So I felt at best dutiful and distinctly sulky. The thing to do was to get it over as quickly as possible.

Mooching along the road to the school I'd forgotten that I had to get into the place. Those old London three-deckers loomed over the area like Bastilles, designed to resist the barbarian natives who surrounded them. What's more, once they'd got you in you couldn't get out because they locked you in. After the second late bell the caretaker did his rounds and turned his key in the narrow single gates pierced in the high walls. Carved in the stone lintels were the words Infants or Girls or Boys. The iron bars of the gates were covered with a sheet of metal to seal you off from the world outside. To get in after the late bell you had to ring and bring the caretaker from his lair, all wheezes, grumbles and frowns. It was the perfect system for making you tremble with guilt, even before you confronted Mr Margolis' glare. When I had the perfect excuse for being late, like a trip to the dentist's, I couldn't shake off the feeling that I'd done something wrong

So I walked down Myrdle Street, passed the sweetshop to the Boys' entrance, a bit disappointed that the turbaned Indian man with his strange little barrow wasn't there any more to sell his tiger nuts, black locust pods, liquorice root, Polish nuts and Indian toffee. I'd have bought some tiger nuts and had a nibble for old time's sake. How quiet that huge school sounded. Somewhere pens were scratching, a child was being ticked off, pages were rustling, chalk was tapping and squealing on a blackboard. A bored boy was probably sitting in my old desk, shuffling his feet. Perhaps Mr Margolis was padding from one classroom door to another, peering through the glass panes. Perhaps a monitor was distributing ink wells or paint pots and was making chinking music. But the great hulk of the school was as quiet as a convent.

I rang the bell. I could hear the lock being fidgeted with and there was the caretaker, looking older and more tired but just as disapproving and testy as ever.

- What do you want?
- I've come to see Mr Margolis.
- What for?

Not an easy question really. Words didn't come easily to the triumphant Matriculated scholar, paying his condescending visit. I cursed my mother's insistence.

- I've come to tell him about my exam results.

He looked at me without moving and stayed silent. It was as though I'd said nothing at all.

- Well, I used to be here, in Mr O'Carroll's class.

He made an impatient noise somewhere at the back of his throat.

- Up the stairs, over there. Top floor.

And he was on his way. I couldn't resist saying loudly enough to his back,

- I should know. Went up them often enough, didn't I?

Some of my cockiness restored, I went up the staircase, passed the Infants on the groundfloor (was the beautiful Miss Gwyllym still there, with all that heaped auburn hair?), past the Girls on the first floor where I had never been. Last lap. Might as well be honest. My mind for a second or two toyed with the notion of turning back. The whole enterprise now seemed ludicrous and distasteful. I was even sketching out a tale to tell my mother. 'He wasn't there. Out on business' or 'He was teaching a class for an absent teacher'.

By now I was at the double doors to the hall. I went through and there he was, at the end of the baize-covered desk, all his accoutrements in their old places, the cane, of course, neatly set out on the table. To the left of him was the glass-fronted cupboard which someone with a nice sense of humour had named The Science Cupboard. The same old mangy bird wing, grey dusty fossils, knobbles of nondescript rock, some bottles with coloured liquids in them, a sloughed snake-skin, a little stuffed rodent, threadbare beyond identification.

The whole length of the hall between him and me. I hadn't got half way and was already out of countenance. I fetched up in front of the dais and the desk, and steeled myself to cope with the pince-nez. Who makes the first move, I wondered. Him, surely. He must greet me in some way or another, if only to ask me my business. By now I didn't quite know what to do with myself. I wanted to put my hands in my pockets and look at the tips of my shoes. I wanted to lean against something or sit down but I knew I shouldn't and couldn't. A silence came down on us and I had no choice throughout but to clench my fists and, unbearably, to look him in the eye. And so I waited and waited and waited. Mr Margolis moved his head very slowly from side to side. Finally he spoke.

- Don't remember the name but a troublesome boy, a troublesome boy.

All the old terrors gripped my guts. I shrivelled to ten-year-old size. Had he ordered me at that moment to put out my hand, mesmerised, I'd have done it. Such is my memory of that moment that I can tell you absolutely nothing about what followed - all, all totally erased from my record.

Kleptomania

I became a thief at eight or nine years old. Up to then I'd gone straight. I don't think I'd stolen a thing. That can't be quite right. I'd taken a cheese cake or two from the larder under the area grating next to the coal or a few Bourbon biscuits on the way back from the grocer's. But they don't count, do they? My booba or my mother would not have called it stealing - naughtiness, perhaps. Furthermore, I didn't have any criminal yearnings at the time. I didn't lie in my bed at night plotting little raids on Mrs Abrams' sweetshop nor how to lift a toy from Danziger's. When I found out that Les took money from his mother's purse from time to time - he let it out in a braggart mood - I was horrified. I got a penny a week pocket money but he had a shilling in his hand, twelve weeks' worth at one go. So when I became a thief it was a new way of life, sudden, absorbing, spiced with pure joy. I went on regular expeditions and looked forward to them, even more than going to the pictures at the Rivoli on Saturday afternoons with Solly. I think I am entitled to say that I wasn't so much a thief as a kleptomaniac. I haven't checked that meaning of that behaviour in the psychology books. You look it up and judge for yourself. But maniac I certainly was for a while. I didn't sell what I stole. I didn't show my loot to friends in a secret huddle. I didn't gloat over it privately like the misers in stories, but I stole, passionately, platonically, piously, unreasonably.

Where did I steal from? Not from Spiegelhalter's jewellery shop, I can tell you. Woolworths. Where else? The one at Gardiners Corner. It had opened just recently and for us kids it was pure magic. We wandered round bemused in the midst of the liveried decor. The awe soon wore off, so much so that nicking began and was developed by real dare-devils into a pilfering spree. No one got arrested, clapped into irons and sent to Borstal for a million years. It was a sort of secret underground club. I heard rumours of it on the grapevine. Then one day Davy came over to me in the playground, stood alongside me and gave me a little nudge.

- Here, he said, look at this.

Dave wasn't too badly off. His father was a taxi driver who read books between fares and kept a cardboard carton full of them all higgledy-piggledy. Davy had more toys than me, including a clockwork train set. His mother, a solemn, anxious woman, always questioned us closely about where we were going. She was sure that at every street corner dangers waited for us - thugs, crooks, murderers even.

- There's goyim out there who'd steal the whites of your eyes and anti-Semites who'd knock you about just for the pleasure it gives them.

- Leave off, leave off, Millie, Mr Taxi would say. You talk like you're still in Warsaw. So, all the same, where are you two off to?

- Solly said we could play with his meccano.

We'd tumble out of Davy's house and go to the fun fair to watch grown-ups losing money on fruit machines.

And here was Dave breathing down my ear, Take a look at this. In front of my belly he opened his fist. In the middle of his pudgy hand was a brand new silvery penknife. It shone like a jewel. I reached out to touch it and he closed his fist at once.

- Keep your hands off. Chup nisht.
- Be a sport. Let's have another look.
- You want it? You do, don't you?
- How many blades?
- Gimme tuppence for it and you'll find out.
- Where d'you get it? You nicked it. You nicked it. Where from?
- Woollies. Tuppence.

His mother would have had a fit, certain that Davy would be put away for ever. Anyway, I didn't have tuppence. If I had I'd have cheerfully parted with it for that shiny little penknife but I was in the ha'penny, at most penny, class. Most of us were. Davy was. He was never going to find a receiver amongst us. Weeks later I saw him sharpening a pencil with it.

Whenever I went into Woolworths I tried to imagine Dave going about his business, reaching out for this and that but I couldn't see it somehow. He was a good boy in class, or good enough. Mr Mitchell never shouted at him or made him kneel, touching the wall with his nose. In the street he backed off our modest hooliganisms, riding a few yards at the back of the coalman's cart, shouting obscenities through Mrs Hamburger's door for taking away our ball, knocking down Ginger. I would stop in front of the counter with penknives and wonder how that good boy Davy had turned himself into a cool gunuf who could pull off his crime undetected.

Even when we were used to it there was a unique allure about Woolworths. It was a world away from the stalls along the Mile End Waste which I used to mooch past. They mostly sold stuff which didn't interest me very much, ladies' shoes, nails and screws, attaché cases, polishes and fly-killer sprays. I did like the stall which sold mini-junk piled into a rusty tarnished heap of all things metallic but it was guarded by an unshaven ogre with filthy fingernails. Once when I picked out a military badge he said, Run along, sonny, with the grimace of a child murderer. Wickhams was our one big store but it was as quiet as a church with most of the goods out of sight and sales people who did a ladies-and-gents act. Yes, madam. No, madam. Not till September, madam. Yards and yards of dark mahogany counters and unreal display dummies in ridiculous poses. I wouldn't have dared go in without my mother. Woolworths declared itself to the world in large golden letters against a pillar-box red background. Very brash, very seductive. Inside it was cooled down to a pervasive claret. Even the shop assistants, all young women, wore claret uniforms. Woolworths was modern. There was nothing like it in the whole of the Whitechapel Road except for the new chromium lettering on Jacobs' shop front.

A few weeks after not buying Davy's penknife for tuppence, I was in the living room trying to shut out the sound of yet another row between my mother and Auntie Zelda about who hadn't paid for something. They had switched into Yiddish to curse the better. My mother kept her end up, of course, but by now I knew just how things were with her, a woman with two kids and no source of income, living off the other adults in that swarming house. As always I crept out and across the road to Solly's place. He wasn't in. So in an aimless zigzag I dragged my feet into New Road, past Dr Sachs' surgery where his vast, unreal St Bernard was on the step as usual, steeped in profound melancholy. On past the Jewish day-nursery with its barred windows and little blue-overalled babies pressed against the bars, snotty-nosed and crying. On past the bakers where I could have bought an enormous piece of bread pudding for a ha'penny but I'd already spent it that morning on sherbet. I got to Whitechapel Road and turned left towards Gardiners Corner. Gardiners Corner! Woolworths! I'd do a turn or two, touching anything I liked in that garden of delights. I started walking properly, past the Foundation School, the Yiddish Theatre, the Salvation Army, the Jewish Reading Room, the old bell foundry, Whitechapel Church and its gravestones and then, under the gold letters, Woolworths.

I made my way over to the counters next to the wall, cheap little tools, some flowery china and then the toys. I found myself standing in front of rows and rows of small scale farmyard animals and farm workers with pitchforks and yokel smocks, railwaymen pushing trolleys, nurses with red crosses, policemen, postmen. I shuffled sideways, scarcely looking at them, to be with my favourites, the soldiers, rank after rank of them, guardsmen, grenadiers, lancers in brilliant colours and plain khaki infantry, mostly frozen in mid-stride with shouldered rifles and some intriguing ones firing from a kneeling or prone position. I always lingered over the two rows of hussars with their cockaded black fur hats. My brother Laurie had signed up for the 11th Hussars when he was sixteen. Who ever heard of a Jewish boy running off to join the army? He ran away from home and lied about his age. He'd already run away from my father in America, worked his way across the Atlantic on a merchant ship and turned up at the already crammed house in Nelson Street. I suppose he must have sized things up and taken a way out. But of all things, the army, and the Cossacks, at that. For my mother it was heartbreak and political shame at the same time. He sent a picture of himself looking heroic in full dress uniform, with his hand on a huge shining sword hilt, festooned with white cord. He had written on the back, 'Show this to Harold and see if he recognises me'. I was thrilled. Idiot. My mother cried over it as she did when we saw him off at Tilbury for India and every time his letters came. We never saw him again.

But the soldiers. They gleamed in front of me. I picked one up, looked at it and put it back. Then another. Then another. I felt electric but calm. Then I picked up one more, a horseguard with a silver helmet, white plume, breastplate and black thigh boots. I held it poised over the counter. I wanted it very badly. The shop assistant was a few yards along. She half turned away as she wrapped something for a customer. An old lady next to me was choosing farm animals and saying to herself, Goats. Why no goats? A farm with no goats. Without any rush, almost dreamily, I moved my arm down to my side and closed my fist over my guardsman. I drifted away and through the store. Exhilarated, I went back home. I carefully wrapped my soldier in a piece of newspaper and put him in my trouser pocket. Later that day my mother said, Bella's making liver rissoles. She says you can go over to her place. I was off to The Buildings, a skinny tenement block fifty yards down the road. The staircase up to Bella Aaronson's top flat always reeked of burnt feathers and discarded guts which came from the slaughtering of chickens in the basement. I tried to hold my breath all the way up. Only something as magnetic as the Aaronsons would have hauled me through the stink. Their tenement was so small you moved around it only by squeezing against the furniture but it was a happy place, full of loud voices and laughter. My mother found a dozen ways of getting me over there when the tensions of our overcrowded house began to boil over. The Aaronsons seemed to cope with their overcrowding quite easily. Bella was my mother's closest friend and fellow Communist. They marched side by side wearing red kerchieves on demonstrations. The family was clever beyond belief. Ezra was already at Cambridge, Josh in the sixth form and Eva in the second form of Raynes Foundation School. Mr Aaronson sat playing the mandolin, inventing things and reading the Marxist classics. Josh was making a wireless. He used to take me to watch him playing rugby. I wished I could live in that feudless home, never mind the stink on the staircase.

So I rushed over to The Buildings. Just before I reached the bottom of the stairs I saw that, where the wall met the pavement, the mortar had fallen away and left a black hole. I knelt down and discovered that my junior hand could just get into it. It was bigger than I expected, a little cave. I took my guardsman out of my pocket, peeled off the newspaper and pushed him into the hole. Then I went on up to the mandolin music and liver rissoles. In bed that night I could see my guardsman safe in his dark quarters. No one in the whole world knew about him except me. The following day I didn't feel the least bit tempted to let anyone into my secret.

A few days later I was in big trouble with Mr Mitchell. My division sums drooped messily down the page and were wrong.

- If you make a nought look like a six, what d'you expect?

Mr Mitchell was getting ratty. In Practical Drawing the shading on my cone was too furry and in the wrong place. In the afternoon I couldn't remember where Vasco da Gama had been. There were other lapses. At four o'clock Mr Mitchell said,

- Did you leave your brains at home today? And don't scowl at me. You better pull your socks up, Rosen, or you'll be for it.

Which was sufficiently vague to be full of menace. After tea I headed towards Gardiners Corner and the soldiers, cheering up as I went. I came away with another one but it took longer this time because the young woman behind the counter was too close and looking straight at me. I had to take a couple of turns round the shop before I saw her dealing with a customer. This time I moved fast. The soldier was in my pocket in an instant. I left the shop and went straight back to the hole in the wall, put him beside my guardsman then up I went to Bella. Every few days I made another raid. There was nothing very clever about my tactics, in fact they never varied. I can't see why I was never caught and disgraced.

I kept going back to the hole in the wall and installing the latest recruit. I let my blind fingers touch the hidden soldiers but I never took one out, let alone a handful which I might have furtively played with. I could have risked storing them at home in a shoe box, perhaps, behind the old encyclopaedias in the dark cupboard on the landing and then I could have put them on parade on the floor when the house was empty. I could have trusted Solly and we could have played for hours in the gloomy old shed in his back yard behind the shop, where we had made ships from wooden boxes and fenced with cardboard rolls. Solly would have loved it. I don't think I could have tried Davy's hucksterering in the playground. I didn't give those possibilities a moment's thought. My soldiers were often in my mind which took me into their burrow and rejoiced in their being there and in the prospect of new recruits. Bliss. My hole was beginning to fill up and I was wondering what to do about it once it was full. I hadn't reached a solution. It didn't cross my mind that I might rest content with my little army. Then one early evening I came back with a kneeling rifleman and as I put him in the hole I knew at once there was something appallingly wrong. I moved my hand about. The hole was empty. Not one left. My heart thumped. I dropped to the pavement and sat with my back to the wall. I put my head on my arms and cried my eyes out. I didn't go up to see Bella and the others. I haven't the faintest idea what I did with my last soldier. It didn't matter. I had given up the whole joyous enterprise.

Mr Old was a never-smiling man who came out from his neck in all directions. His acid-holed brown lab coat made him look like a grocer. Not like the biology teacher who always wore a freshly-laundered and starched white coat like a hospital doctor. I wouldn't be sneering at Mr Old's brown coat if, even at this distance, I didn't still feel spiteful about him. We didn't like each other from the beginning. Yet he should have had a lot going for him. He had his own little manor over the gateway of an old blackened building separate from the main school. It's now listed as an eighteenth century schoolhouse. It's still there, a Bangladeshi Arts Centre. His fiefdom consisted of a laboratory, a preparation room and a classroom which uniquely was a little lecture theatre rising steeply in tiered levels, on each of which was an unbroken length of wooden bench and long oak boards dotted with white inkwells on which we rested our notebooks and carved yet another set of initials. Compared with the single-seater desks in the other classrooms this was a paradise of possibilities for nudging, elbowing, ankle-kicking, note-passing and trafficking. When we arrived for lessons there was a clattering din from our shoes on the wooden floorboards and steps as we rushed for favoured positions near the windows, up the top at the back, at the ends of the rows, but never in the middle. Schloch, we called him, a Jewish nickname inherited from the mockery of previous generations (would it be lummox in English?).

At the front of the class down in the well he had his own teak bench with sink and bunsen burner, where he would conduct the demonstration of the day, talking to himself, and we would wait for one of his many cock-ups: the brown ring would not make its mystical appearance, the glowing splint would not burst into flame, the colour of the litmus paper would be dubious. We would cheer and yaboo. Even when all went as planned we would pretend it hadn't. As the wine-coloured permanganate of potash streamed up the beaker, across the top and down the sides as it was supposed to, You can see, he would say, just how the heat is circulating in the water.

- No, no, we would shout. Where? What heat? It's only making the water red, that's all.

- Stand up, Rosen, say that again.

- Me? Why me? I didn't say a word.

- Take a hundred lines.

The fountain experiment didn't fountain, the dessicator didn't dessicate. When hydrogen sulphide was finally produced in the Kipp's apparatus after several false starts we were supposed to confirm that it smelled liked rotten eggs. Some of the lads pretended that they were overcome with the fumes, groaning on their way to unconsciousness, and one bright spark shouted out, Who farted? Disgusting! Schloch dictated,

- Hydrogen sulphide is a colourless, poisonous gas with a smell like rotten eggs.

- Poisonous! said the fainters, poisonous! I'm going to report this!

- It burns in the air with a lilac flame, forming -

- Lilac flame? We didn't see any lilac flame. You didn't burn it.

- We'll be doing that in the lab in the fourth year.

- Not me! I'm doing physics next year. No farts in physics.

There had been a time when science seemed to me to hold some promise. In a rare moment Schloch had gone off into a monologue about perpetual motion and how scientists had tried for millenia to achieve it and all had failed. I went away and found myself thinking about it. I was stirred and challenged. I sat at home, scribbling and diagramming in my rough notebook. I thought I'd cracked the problem in a simple and elegant manner, all on the basis of one lesson on the apparent loss of weight of bodies in water. It went like this. You'd start with a balance beam and from each end you'd suspend exactly the same weight but one of the weights would be submerged in a beaker of water. It wouldn't stay there because immediately it would rise because of its apparent loss of weight. The beam would tilt. But then it would be equal in weight again and therefore drop into the beaker of water. So the beam would go up and down for ever and ever. On a big enough scale, I reasoned, it could be harnessed for all sorts of purposes, irrigation, for example. I came rushing into the next science lesson.

- Sir, I've done it, I've done it.

Schloch looked baffled.

- Done what?
- Perpetual motion, sir. I've invented it.

I showed him the sketches in my notebook with their crucial up-and-down arrows and gabbled out my explanation. He took the notebook and studied it with great care, I thought. I was waiting for his praise, of course, but much more for shared excitement. I looked up at his indecipherable face. Then he handed me back my notebook.

- It wouldn't work.

Just that. Nothing more. I might have said, Sir, sir, we could rig it up in the lab. Just to see.

Science in me had taken a terrible wound and begun to die. It never recovered.

I was persuaded that whenever collective insubordination broke out I was the one selected for blame and punishment. Mark said, It's because of your red hair. Sticks out a mile. But he was the only one to agree that I had some sort of case. It soon reached the point where in almost every lesson, after about ten minutes, Schloch would say,

- Rosen, out. Stand under the second lamp on the landing.

God knows how many torturing hours of boredom I spent on that landing and how much of the chemistry syllabus I missed. Schloch and I were soon sworn enemies. There was one Wednesday afternoon when I was playing football for a school team and when I got back my pals, killing themselves with laughter, reported that there'd been a subversive, very noisy huddle at the back of the room, just before the lesson was about to begin. Schloch came in and shouted,

- Rosen, you again. Out, under the second lamp on the landing.

They had all pretended to search for me under the benches.

- Come out of it, Rosen. Mr Old wants a word with you.

When it dawned on him what was afoot his purple fury silenced them. At the next lesson I went up to him, aimiably solicitous.

- Sorry I didn't make it to your last lesson, sir. I hear you were looking for me. I knew you'd miss me.

- Rosen, he said, any more of your cheek and I'm sending

you straight to the Head.

I knew he wouldn't. But that was all a year ahead when I was taller than Schloch and could manage him with words and make him turn from me, speechless. But here in the third year I yearned for revenge. At least I think now that's why I took up the criminal life again in a strictly kleptomaniac style.

The door to the prep room opened onto the penitential landing. It had another door which opened directly into the little lecture theatre. A day came when I decided to risk all and take a look inside. It was, after all, Schloch's lair and strictly private. The handle turned quietly enough and I was in. It was beautiful. One corner was snugly domestic - a small oak desk, on it a pipe and tobacco tin, a college photo of a football team in which I could spot a bright and unwearied Mr Old. His overcoat and gown hung from a couple of clothes hooks on the wall. The curved teacher's chair had a green velvet cushion on the seat and a fine china teapot and tea cup and saucer sat on a wooden tray together with a started packet of biscuits. I don't know what full-time thieves feel when they first soft-foot into a room which still bears the imprints of a living person. But I was for a second or two abashed, ashamed even. This little corner was more human and decent than Schloch had ever seemed in lessons. I could hear the rasp of his voice through the door.

I turned to tip-toe out, and as I did so I took in the rest of the room. There was shelving all round at waist height, littered with a few bunsen burners, clamps, beakers, flasks, test-tube racks, retorts, rusty tripods and rubber tubing - as random as a junk shop. Above the shelving were narrower shelves with bottles, jars and small boxes, everything in perfect order and labelled neatly. I moved towards them. I plucked off a shelf a little brown glass jar labelled 'Iodine' and slid out of the prep room to take up my station under the second lamp. The hour went faster now and from time to time I shook the bottle and listened to the dry little crystals making rustling music. At home I went into the backroom kitchen where there was an open fire by the side of a black oven. When it got dark, I tipped a few of the black iodine crystals into my hands and scattered them on the fire. I knew what was going to happen. A very beautiful violet vapour went up the chimney. In a few days I had burned all my stolen goods. On my next raid I stole some silvery white magnesium strips. I knew about them, too, and set light to them in our back yard when no one was about. They burned with a spectacular, intense flame. This was all strictly fireworks and nothing to do with what they call an enquiring mind. They might just as well have been Guy Fawkes Day sparklers.

There was no turning back now. When I was sent out to the second lamp instead of plodding out with dull resignation I began to tingle with the thought of my next pad round the prep room. There was a limit to the safely combustible substances so I began to diversify by lifting small objects, some wire gauze, a bit of rubber tubing and clips, marble chips, charcoal sticks, zinc turnings, calcite crystals. I even chanced the fragility of a little thistle funnel, delicately pretty. Once I had taken these things away and gone home from school I didn't know what to do with them. I didn't want to keep them, that's for sure. I just threw them away. Wrapped in newspaper they all went into the dustbin, except for the thistle funnel, which I loved for its own sake, I mean my sake. I wrapped it in a bit of rag and kept it in my satchel where, by a miracle, it survived.

About a week later Nat was smouldering alongside me in the playground.

- Dunce. Right in front of the whole class. Dunce. A snivelling little dunce, he called me.

- A what?

- A snivelling little dunce. That schmeryl, he don't know enough chemistry to make salt water for pickled cucumbers.

I was a bit surprised at Nat getting so worked up at a piece of routine abuse from Schloch of all people, who threw his insults around with abandon. We were all inured to being called stupid in different ways by most of our teachers. It went with being a teacher, though there were two or three who seemed to manage very well without it. We were from time to time numbskulls, thickheads, ignoramuses, nincompoops and plain fools. Schloch once called me incorrigible and I went round trying to find out what it meant until a fifth former told me it was just a long word meaning dumm. I liked the word and tried to use it when insulting my friends, You're an incorrigible katzenkopf. Anyway, Nat's grumps were a bit odd.

- Ferric. I just said ferric instead of ferrous.

Must have been more to it than that. It seems funny now because Nat went on to take a degree in chemistry and became an acknowledged expert in the history of plastics. He usually came top in chemistry but Schloch was very even-handed in his abuse, meting it out to good and bad students alike. He knew nothing about pride, at least, not ours.

Nat clearly needed cheering up.

- Here, you wanna see something real good? I said impulsively.

I dug out of my satchel the handful of rag and then pulled out the thistle funnel.

- A thistle funnel. That's from the lab. How d'you get hold of it? Show us.

- Don't chup, you'll drop it. Treat it careful.

- You stole it, didn't you? How did you manage to gunver a thing like that?

- It's easy.

I mindlessly opened the floodgates. I spilled out everything, all the secrets of the prep room.

- With a naar like that you could steal the gutgas off his tuchas, the pants off his bum.

- Tell me, said Nat, what do you do with it all? Nowhere in your house where they wouldn't find it. You collecting for a chemistry set?

- Chemistry set! I just get rid of it, throw it away.

- What do you take it for then?

I couldn't answer that really. The question embarrassed me. I had expected him to get some taste of the pure joy of it all. We sat in silence for a bit and then Nat said,

- They could expel you for that. They would, too. And they might even report it to the police. You'd be a criminal.

I took my thistle funnel back and put in my satchel.

- It's a secret, don't forget. Just you and me.

Some hopes! By the next day everyone in the class knew.

- What's on the list today, Al Capone? Concentrated nitric acid?

- Could you gunver for me some Epsom salts or bicarbonate of soda? My father likes them.

Someone did a take-off of Schloch standing in the preparation room, scratching his head and saying, I could swear I put that pipette down here. And that jar of flowers of sulphur, where's it gone? Must ask that evil Rosen if he knows anything about it.

- Here, Rosie, there's a nice little bank just up the road -

I didn't enjoy the wit very much and it soon died down. Sometime afterwards a few of us were standing by the school gates at four o'clock, larking about, and suddenly Barney said,

Kleptomania

- Rosie, get something from the prep room for us.
- Like what?
- Anything, anything.

They jostled round me. I'd become a kind of mascot or champion. I revelled in it.

- Get something really big.
- Really big?
- Yeah, like a tripod or clamp.

I was lifted by their confidence in me, not understanding their vicarious and riskless excitement. I went straight to the wooden steps right by us and up to the landing. I was sure there would be no one about at this time of day. Schloch left at four o'clock sharp. I turned off the landing into the lab. I knew I wouldn't find the heavy iron stuff in the prep room and that there was an iron clamp next to each bunsen burner and sink. I grabbed a clamp, concealed it a bit under my blazer and was soon with my pals by the gate. I got all the admiration I could have hoped for. Barney said,

- You should get a prize for chutzpah. You've got something to give the old iron man next time he's round.
- Where we gonna put it? someone said.

It was 'we' now, was it? I put the clamp on the ground and they stood around it. It looked so outrageously conspicuous that I began to get jumpy. The others looked foolish and were also nervy.

- We'll have to get it back, Barney said.
- Who's going? I asked.
- What a question, said Barney. You're the only one who'll do it. There's no one there, is there?

This was much more than I'd bargained for but I could see there was nothing for it. I picked up the clamp. Up the stairs again, trying to stop the boards from creaking, and then on to the landing. My plan was to put the clamp on the landing and flee but I hesitated. At that very instant, Schloch came out of the prep room in his raincoat and shapeless trilby. He stopped. I prayed and prepared to die. One of my aunt's Yiddish curses went through my mind again and again, 'May God's heat melt him into a candle'. But God's heat did no such thing. He came up to me, bristling so fiercely that I thought he was going to punch me. Instead he grabbed me by the lapel and pushed me to the wall.

- That clamp. How did you get hold of it? You not only

chatter and misbehave in my lessons but you also steal equipment. Incredible. Speak up. This is a very serious matter. The Head will hear about this and your parents. What have you got to say for yourself? Do you know how much this costs, you nasty little specimen? What's your tale?

He hadn't let go of my lapel yet.

- Sir, I said, sir ....I - we found it.

Schloch, of course, didn't believe a word of it but he was struggling to find some way of countering my lie and extracting a confession. He let go of me and burned.

- Found? Found? Are you mad? Is lab equipment littering the school playground?

- But sir, sir, we found it by the school gate just downstairs. You can ask the others. We were larking about when we saw it.

- The others, eh? Just larking about. And they chose you, of all people, to bring it back, the honest one.

- Yes, sir, I said I'd bring it back. Couldn't leave it there.

- No, might have got stolen, is that what worried you? You don't like things being stolen from here, do you? We'll get to the bottom of this, you can be sure of that.

He never did, gott sei dank. But when we were in the lab sometime afterwards, Schloch sent a trusty to get some litmus paper from the prep room and he said,

- Here's the key. Lock the door up after you.

As he spoke I imagined he was looking in my direction. I was probably wrong. I hadn't tried the prep door again anyway and I had lost all appetite for its treasures. Believe it or not, I got a distinction in chemistry in the matriculation exam. I didn't know any chemistry but I had learned a textbook by heart, clamps and all.

Not Becoming A Lawyer

I didn't become a lawyer at sixteen. But then I didn't become a trooper in the 11th Hussars either (though improbably I had a brother who did), nor did I become a bagel seller in Hessel Street market, nor a chazan in a synagogue. And so on. But not becoming a lawyer was something special. To this very day part of me is this not becoming a lawyer.

When I got to the grammar school at eleven years of age, I was not, you should understand, in the business of becoming anything. I had done what my mother expected of me, passed the scholarship, as they used to say in those days. I had got the message from her that the scholarship was very, very important.

- You gotta learn when you do this scholarship you can make a different life. Look at your zeider. He's a clever man. He reads everything, newspapers, Karl Marx, Zangwill - I don't know what. But what is he? A machinist. At seventy he spends his life bent over a sewing machine. A machinist. Never had a chance to be a Foundation School boy, did he? So he's stuck to that machine like he was glued to it. But you, you could be ....

I looked up.

- I could be what?

- Well, you work that out later. You do your scholarship, go to the new school, study, get good marks and then you find out. Look at the Michaelson boy, Aaron. He's a Cambridge college boy now.

I still didn't quite understand what was so important. But it didn't matter. If it was important for her, that was good enough for me. I did my stuff and there I was, a scholarship boy. I had a cap with a lovely badge, a new satchel, and books I could take home. I was dazzled by teachers in gowns and the hall with its timbered ceiling and walls. All that for me was achievement enough. As Mrs Warshaw said to me one day when I'd been a bit cheeky, 'And you're supposed to be a psychollege boy!' which showed I'd got somewhere.

So I had no long-term goals. I wasn't limbering up for a long, long course in deferred gratification. In fact, come to think of it, I was more in the business of short-term gratification, like most of the other boy-wonders in my class. Mind you, I'll admit that a handful of them always worked as though someone was standing next to them with a whip. They crouched over their books, shining with diligence like true Talmudic scholars. Yeshiva bochers! A touch and they would have been rocking to and fro. Some kind of strange engine drove them on to their passionate devotions. Yet, if my memory serves me right, it wasn't a dream of becoming someting really big - a learned rabbi, a writer of books, the owner of a pickle factory, a pioneering psychiatrist, a research chemist. Nor, let me say it, a famous lawyer. They slogged their kishkas out because somewhere out there they had picked up on their antennae the message: either you did business, sold and bought, or you bent over your books and studied. It didn't matter which. And what's more, as they handed in their impeccable homework, I don't think they had in their mind's eye the reward of a studio portrait of themselves capped, gowned and clutching a scroll. They were just being blindly virtuous. We were very busy getting by. We had to learn how to cope with Mr Riley's blind furies. He was a grown man with nice white hair and a white moustache but he could gibber with rage and venom just because a snotty-nosed boy got his sums wrong. Perhaps he was punishing us for having become a teacher. That's not what I thought then, of course. I had come to think of his purple-faced tantrums as the way of the world, the same as Mr Llewelyn's acid mockery, Mr Sansom's profound indifference or Mr Lee's magisterial remoteness - and there were all the others. We had to learn them all, to read them sufficiently well to keep to a minimum all the major disasters - detentions, lines, seeing the Head, and, God forbid, the ultimate indignity, the cane. And then time had to be found for larking about with Manny and Sid. I can't remember exactly what we did except that we laughed a lot of the time and did imitations of our teachers. We spent hours playing football with a tennis ball in the playground, knocking the hell out of our shoes. At home we listened to the grown-ups talking forever and forever of the tailoring and the sweat shop guvnors, of politics, strikes, Mosley's Black Shirt invasions and memories of der Heim in Poland, or Russia, or Lithuania. We walked round the neighbourhood, beating the bounds of the ghetto, up the Whitechapel Road and the Mile End Waste for chips, sarsparilla and the occasional salt-beef sandwich. And we went to the pictures to see *Metropolis, Michael Strogonoff,* and *Moby Dick* and the Barrymores in everything at the Rivoli and the Palaceum. Homework we were sure swallowed up all our spare time but somehow we squeezed in a lot of things between homeworks, nothing very improving though.

Perhaps we kept the career thing to ourselves, unnerved by the unemployed on every corner and the tailors on short time, and the schmutter trade on its last legs. There were tales of boys who'd left our school with Honours in Matric who were serving in shops or making tea in offices. We tried not to hear such stories, or put their misfortune down to bad luck. Anyway, things would be different by the time we were sixteen.

Perhaps it was talked about in our homes.

- The Stern boy is a medical student at the London Hospital. You should just see him. Looks like a doctor already.

- Doesn't matter what you do, don't go into the tailoring. Slavery. Better be like a goy and work on the roads. Furrier, dressmaker, it's all the same.

- I heard from Mrs Feidleman that if you take a little exam same time you take your Matric you can get a good job with the London County Council. Bessie's boy, Mark, did it.

- Do me a favour! Stay on till he's sixteen? He can leave at fourteen, fifteen, and get the same lousy job he'd get at sixteen.

- That boy's so clever he could be anything, anything. So what's he talk to me about all of a sudden? Learning to play the saxophone! To play the saxophone!

Buzz, buzz. Doing Caesar's Gallic Wars (what else?) in Latin when I was fifteen had nothing to do with getting a job. For that matter it didn't seem to me to have anything to do with anything else either. I must say, though, there were for me excellent, disreputable reasons for liking the fact of doing Latin. It made you one with those splendid young goyim in the public school stories who shouted 'Cave!' when a teacher was sighted and whose teachers in Latin class said, 'Construe, Carruthers Minor'. They never, never talked about their careers.

By the time I was fifteen I'd managed to keep my head above water. What more could anyone ask? My end of term reports were almost respectable but when I took them home there'd be a few barbs which would make my mother jumpy. 'Not very assiduous except at irrelevant chatter'.

- Course, 'irrelevant chatter'. You see, big mouth? said my mother. Just like your uncle Bernie, so busy putting in your two ha'porth you don't hear nothing.

- But I came fifth in his lousy subject.

- I told you, I told you, she said, half crying. Trouble with you, you can't listen - to me, or your zeider, or your booba, not even your teacher. You're gonna end up as a felling hand.

There was usually enough to console her by the time she reached the Head's non-committal 'A reasonable term's work'.

- See? I said, taking advantage of her doubt. 'Reasonable'. What more could you want?

But it was clear that all those expert judges of schoolboy genius and talent did not see me as headed for high renown and gilt lettering on the Honours Board. But my mother still nursed her high ambitions and made me decidedly uneasy. So I didn't dwell on it. From my undemanding point of view I had managed well enough in school exams and was now steeling myself for the Fifth Form and the most important thing in the world, Matric. We all plunged into the preparation and it blotted out the universe. In the midst of all the pathetic swotting and the slightly hysterical threats from teachers ('You'll fail, you dunderhead, if you don't learn the notes on valency!'), Suddenly we took a bit of time out to talk about jobs. I hope you noticed I have just started calling them jobs. Careers! They have careers teachers nowadays, don't they? Our teachers never so much as soiled their lips with the word 'careers'. They behaved as though this was none of their business. We never expected it of them. There was no question of any of them coming up to me in the corridor, putting an arm round my shoulder, and saying,

- What are you going to do, old chap? I mean, what are you going in for? Must have thought about it by now. Accountancy? Medicine? Architecture? Civil Service? Er - Law, perhaps?

I don't think they cared a scrap. What's more, I don't blame them. They had their work cut out getting us through exams. And they knew, as we only sensed, that most of us would end up as clerks in the City less than half a mile away, where they demanded good Matric results from aspiring office boys.

We would get into little huddles by a radiator or in the playground and talk about what we called work, as in homework, schoolwork, bookwork. It was all a matter of plotting and planning to counter the cunning of examiners with our own wiles. Despairing of passing in Chemistry because of a hopeless teacher and an out-of-date textbook, Manny and I pooled our cash and bought a crammers' book, *Littler's School Certificate Chemistry Notes*. We learned it by heart, testing each other out for hours on end. I got a distinction in Chemistry, never having seen most of the substances I wrote about nor conducted, or even observed, any of the experiments. That kind of swotting was full-time work. A nasty smell of anxiety hung in the air and we infected each other with our fears. The evil worm of competition took over our psyches. When Frumkin started saying knowledgeably, 'You gotta know about the differences between Dissenters, Puritans and Protestants' we should have found that very funny: he was an unbarmitzvahed atheist and couldn't have told you the difference between the United Reformed Synagogue and the Hassidim. Instead we lost our nerve and shouted that it wasn't on the syllabus. Secretly we knew he was miles ahead of us with his revision and we hated him for it. All the same, better look up the stuff about Dissenters and so on.

From time to time the other kind of work came up - as in factory work, manual work, clerical work. We were very confused and profoundly ignorant. We didn't know what anybody actually did, except in those jobs we didn't want - tailoring and being shop assistants. Ben's brother was the manager of a cinema somewhere in Dalston and used to stand in the foyer in evening dress and control the queues. Bit of a pantomime really. Jacob had an uncle who went from door to door, buying old jewellery.

- What's he do with it? we wanted to know.
- Sells it, I suppose.
- Makes a mint, I bet.
- He makes a living, said Jacob.

At home my mother was doing her best to make sure that my nose was in my books every waking hour undistracted by Solly and Len playing football in the street and chatting up the girls in front of Gilbovsky's. I stopped going to the boys' club for chess and table tennis, to Victoria Park running track, to the pictures to see Claudette Colbert and Clark Gable, not because I couldn't have spared an hour or two but because any pleasure would have been stained with guilt.

One day (could it have been early in the summer term?) Cousin Leslie arrived at the house. This was an event which did not occur very often. Great aunts and uncles, yes. Cousins of all sorts, yes. They were frequent unannounced visitors. No one had a diary to pencil them in. There was no phone to take a call. Suddenly they were on the doorstep. From the cellar my booba took pickled herrings, pickled cucumbers, chopped liver, calves' foot jelly, perhaps, and one of the kids was hurried off to the corner shop for Bourbon biscuits. Lemon tea was made. The visitors settled down and spent hours revisiting the past. The kids listened avidly. I remember listening to the tale of my cousin Noah, educated and well-heeled, who became a Special in the General Strike.

- The momser, said my zeider, a Special, worse than a blackleg. Next time he came round I told him there on the doorstep to clear off back to Hendon and join the Cossacks. And you know what? You won't believe this, three years later, by my life so sure, he had to run off to South America. Sarah said he gambled with other people's money. Just right for a strike breaker, eh? A few more pennies for the miners he couldn't stand.

And always the story of deaf Aunt Rifca. In the middle of a rambling account of my great-grandmother's journey from Odessa to Newcastle (she thought she was going to London) Rifca said, 'Don't be silly, he lived with us for twenty years!' This massive non-sequitur was always trotted out from then on when somebody didn't stick to the point.

But here suddenly was Cousin Leslie, something quite different. He was one of those few wealthy relatives who existed on the very fringes of our lives but occasionally one of them would descend on us out of the blue and set the house a-flutter, make us lose confidence in our pickled herrings and our Yiddish and our family legends. Cousin Leslie was already moving along the dark passage into the living room. My sister told me a short while back, when I was talking about these events, that his full name was Leslie Sunshine. I loved that. You'll see why.

Cousin Leslie was a lawyer, more exactly, a solicitor, and he ran his office somewhere near the City. To all of us he was rich, clever, prestigious, could-pass-for-English-gent Cousin Leslie.

None of us could speak like him. He sounded official. And he looked like those ganzer machers on the platform on Speech Day. He was shiny bald, plump in the face, wore gold-rimmed specs and a beautifully cut, perfect suit (if we knew how to judge anything it was how to judge a suit) and he smiled out of it all the time. He went round being nice to everyone. At one point he came over to me.

- You got a scholarship to Grammar School, didn't you? Must be in your Matric year by now, am I right? What subjects are you taking? What's your favourite subject? Do you get good marks?

Don't ask me what I answered. I was over-awed and I mumbled. By this time my mother had inserted herself behind his left ear. He turned to her now.

- Ah, Rose (no one ever called her Rose: she was Rosie to the family), I hear the boy's in his Matric year, eh? How's he doing, would you say? Going to get good results?

- He's a scholar, said my mother, with a conviction on that score that I had never heard before.

- What more could you want? If he's a scholar he's going to get good results. Tell me now, what's he going to do? You must put your mind to that, you know. No use leaving it to the last moment. You've got to weigh up the possibilities. Have you thought about that?

- He could stay on, my mother said, but did not sound very convinced herself. Small wonder. I hadn't heard a word about this possibility.

- Mmmmm, said Cousin Leslie, as though my mother had said something implausible, perhaps even silly. Have you thought about Law, Rose?

- Well, no. Not Law. No, I haven't. Nor have you, she said, turning to me. You haven't thought about Law either, have you? Not Law.

All those Jewish jokes about my son, the lawyer! I had already heard and even told a few. But this was getting serious. What exactly was Cousin Leslie getting at? I knew that in those days you had to be articled to someone in a practice, a sort of posh apprenticeship, and you paid a lot for the privilege. If Cousin Leslie was making this proposal, he also knew we didn't have a penny.

- Listen, he said to me again. When you get your results - that's in August, isn't it? - if they're good, something better than a row of bare passes, get in touch with me. Do you understand? You'll find me in the phone book, Rose.

He was gone soon after. My mother and I looked at each other. I was overjoyed, excited and a bit confused.

- You know what he means, don't you? Does he have to write it on a piece of paper for you? He's a man of few words. He'll take you on and we won't have to pay. Nothing. You're going to be a lawyer. Just get your Matric and that's it.

Cousin Leslie Sunshine had worked a miracle. I could get back to my books with my future settled. It was, I felt, a decidedly grand one. I hadn't had to lift a finger and I was almost a lawyer already. What did a solicitor do? What would I be doing to start with? I hadn't the faintest idea and I didn't give a damn.

Don't think I went back to school and bragged about it. There are unwritten rules about such things. All the same, at those rare moments when our chatter turned to jobs, I'd drop into the conversation that I was going to become a lawyer. At first they only half believed me, if at all.

- A lawyer, said Clever-Dick Monty, you've got my custom already for when I take up a life of crime. Mind you, I don't think you look the part with all that red hair and bad jokes. Anyway, where's the money going to come from?

But they came round soon enough and it gradually became part of the wisdom of the group that Rosen was going to become a lawyer just like Manny was going to do science. It felt very good, even better than doing Latin.

I said before that our teachers never showed the least interest in what we might be doing after we left their care but there was one exceptional occasion. One day when the exams were terrifyingly near our Form Master, Mr Lee, came into the room with a large official sheet of paper.

- Now, he said, I've been asked by the Head to fill in this form which will give him details of what you propose to do after completing your matriculation examinations.

Hands shot up all over the place.

- What if you don't know, sir?
- I haven't made my mind up, sir.
- Depends on the results, sir, said Reuben. Doesn't make sense. Chancing his arm he added, What's the Head going to do with it all, sir?

Mr Lee raised his hand.

- Common sense has gone out of the window here today.

We pretended to look for it, craning our necks.

- And good manners, said Mr. Lee. It's very simple. If you know, say so. If you don't know, say so. If you are not sure, say something like, 'Possibly this or that'. Is that clear?

Reuben whispered noisily to me that if we didn't know what they were doing this for we shouldn't say a word. He was always red hot on civil liberties - in principle.

- Reuben, said Mr Lee, if you find all that too much for your brain to take, you can have a private consultation at the end of this lesson.

Reuben, who'd had a good run for his money, subsided irritably into his desk.

Mr Lee went through the class list.

- Abrams, Berkoff, Cohen, Cernowitz, Dolinsky, Danziger, Frumkin, Friedman, Greenspan ....There were a lot of not sures and a few surprises. Someone said he was going to Regent Street Polytechnic (to do what? why hadn't he said?). Levin said he was going to stay on in the Sixth Form which made Mr Lee look over his glasses for a long few seconds. My turn came.

- Law, I said, loudly and boldly.

Mr Lee pretended he had not heard.

- Law, I repeated, staying calm.

- Keeping it or breaking it? he asked.

The arse-lickers fell about. My friends gently hissed.

Later in the playground, I must admit, there was quite a group who were chanting, 'Keeping it or breaking it? Keeping it or breaking it?'

It was all over and forgotten soon enough and it was back to exams. I sweated with the others through the sweltering July days. I joined the post-mortems after each paper.

- Bloody swindlers! No question on the Factory Acts.

- But Schloch said there'd be no question on bromine.

- What did you get for question seven?

I had my worst moment in Algebra. I put my pen down in despair and listened to a barrel organ in the street below playing the Valeta, a tune my mother loved to dance to. Soothed, I went back to the paper and found it more do-able than before. Everyone who's ever taken an exam knows all this and still has nightmares about it.

August came and we assembled in the hall to hear our results. I'd done it. Some distinctions, some scrapes. I'd got a decent Matric. I was going to be a lawyer. I rushed home with the news. My mother did not hesitate.

- Phone Leslie. Phone Leslie. Now. Here's the number.

She pushed some coppers and a scrap of paper into my hand. I ran to the kiosk outside the Sussex Steam Laundry and stood getting my breath back and carefully rehearsed my words. I dialled. It was a secretary.

- Can I speak to Mr Sunshine, please?
- Who's calling?
- Tell him it's Harold. I'm his cousin.

She brought him to the phone.

- It's me, Harold, Leslie. I've done it. My Matric. I've passed it. I've just heard, up at the school.
- Yes, he said. He sounded a little puzzled and not particularly pleased.

I stumbled on.

- You remember? You told me to get in touch. To let you know if I got my Matric. I mean if I got good results. Well, I did. Shall I tell them to you?
- Not just now. Some other time. I'm glad you did well. Very impressive. Rose must be absolutely delighted. Congratulations and good luck.

And Cousin Leslie Sunshine put the phone down on me. For ever.

Cribs

I was sitting there so bored I could have cried. I'd finished the arithmetic paper and was waiting for Mr Powell to declare the exam over and done with. Following the order of the time, if you finished before the Head rang the bell in the hall, you sat there in total silence doing nothing. Could have let us have a book from the cupboard, I thought. Like *King of the Golden River* which we'd started reading in class, and which was nice to handle, bright red and gilt lettering. It was all good practice for something or other - the army? prison? - but an excruciating strain for a ten-year-old. All you could do was look round the room to see how the others were making out or study the flaking map of the world and the faded pictures, '*When did you last see your father?*', '*The Fighting Temeraire*' and '*Napoleon on the Bellerophon*'. Most of the others had their arms curled round their papers and their heads almost buried inside them. This was to stop someone nearby from cheating. Bit of a laugh in Benjy's case. He would be lucky to get a couple of sums right and he would certainly not finish more than a quarter of the paper. Yet there he was like a miser over his hoard. He might not be very good at arithmetic but he had mastered the ethics of scholarly behaviour. I think he believed that if he only adopted the correct physical posture he would join the elect. Getting sums wrong shows a certain lack of fibre but cheating we all knew was a moral disorder of a much more reprehensible kind. We knew this, not because we were able to take in all that moral business but because we could tell from the scale of the outrage of our teachers when confronted by some protesting little cheat that copying an answer from someone else's paper or writing something in the palm of your hand or smuggling in a tiny scrap of paper was a crime against the social fabric itself. 'Cheating is a kind of stealing', said Mr Powell. 'It's stealing knowledge'. Dicky Kahn thought that was funny. 'So mein kind', he said later in a Yiddisher momma's voice, you mustn't be a knowledge gunuf. Same as in Woolworth's, tatele.

In the morning assembly after a suitable run-up of prayers and a hymn, Mr Margolis has sketched out the ground rules.

- Tomorrow you all start your exams. This will be the most important day of the year. You will be given full instructions by your teachers but I want to say something special to you. As you all know, if you copy or even try to copy from another boy's paper, that is cheating. All your work must be your own. Never try to ask someone else for an answer and don't attempt to give one. Anyone doing any of these things will be severely punished.

Some of us glanced at the canes in brine in the aquarium. Mr Margolis had used one of his special voices, not the more-in-sorrow-than-in-anger one, not the bespoke sarcastic one for a shaking criminal hauled to the front of the hall, but the high solemn one of an Old Testament prophet warning of a plague or the risk of God's displeasure. I can't say I was following very closely. One way to avoid getting shaky and afraid was not to listen. In any case I didn't think any of this concerned me very much. Cheating wasn't my particular line of crime. Mr Margolis was now taking one of his long pauses. His gaze went to and fro and through us to let the dire threat sink in. And then he started up again.

- Now when you're doing your exams you'll stay out of trouble if you keep your eyes on your papers and don't look to right or left. Like that idiot at the back is doing right now. Yes, you with the uncombed hair.

And here he suddenly bellowed,

- Get out! Get out of my sight! On the landing. I'll deal with you later.

The uncombed one, for us a hero, a martyr, slouched out.

- You see? he went on, there's always one. Make sure it isn't you. Another thing. You mustn't make signs of any kind to another boy. Don't pull silly faces. Don't make lip movements. Don't signal with your hands. It's all cheating. Cheating, you understand. We are not going to tolerate any of it. Not a flicker of it. There will be no cheats in my school.

Now that I'd finished the paper there was certainly no need for me to cheat from the arm-curlers around me. Then I noticed Dickie Kahn. He was just across the aisle from me and he too had finished. He was leaning back in his seat, arms behind his neck, and staring at the ceiling. I tried to catch his eye and failed. That was a risky thing to do. All classes in the Big Boys were examined at the same time. The classroom doors were fastened wide open so that Mr Margolis could monitor the whole exercise from the hall and prowl round the classes to root out the slightest irregularity and in particular, cheating. The open doors were also to impress upon us that this was one of the big ritual moments of the year. They also made us feel more exposed, out in the open. Given the surveillance of our own teachers they would otherwise have seemed foolishly unnecessary. All in all, by the time we'd started examinations only wild desperation or advanced idiocy would have made anyone try it on.

I looked across at Dickie Kahn. This time I did catch his eye. Catching an eye was, I suppose, within the meaning of the act. But I did. And he let the faintest hint of a smile cross his face. There were just a few minutes to go. He silently mouthed the word, 'Finished?' I mimed the answer, 'Hours ago'. As I did so, a great terrifying shout hit my ear like a punch. It was Mr Margolis who had spied me from the open door, rushed in and bellowed into my ear, 'Cheat! You were cheating! Mr Powell, this boy was openly cheating. Now, cheat, get out and stand in front of my desk in the hall. We know what to do with cheats here.' He was dragging me from my desk and pushing me to the door, past Mr Powell who looked a bit upset. Possessively, he didn't like one of his pupils in big trouble.

Mr Margolis made short work of me. My fear and sense of huge injustice had already set me crying and I made one spluttering attempt at a protest. Much good it did me. Out came the cane and I got two fierce whacks on each hand. Mr Margolis led me back to my class and the others took in my tears and misery. He led me right up to my desk. There was the arithmetic paper I had finished with such assurance. With a red pencil he scored a punitive diagonal line across one page after another and then he wrote on the first page, '0 marks. CHEATING'. I'd been in some scrapes before but nothing like this. And there was worse to come. Every one of the papers I had already done was given a nought mark and I came bottom of the class when minutes before I had thought that Dickie and I were competing to be top. The disaster darkened my world. I had in a way bought the cheating thing and had come to believe there was something despicable about it. But now a thousand Mr Margolises would never convince me that justice had been done and been seen to be done. Mr Margolis had devoured and digested me and it had nothing to do with cheating as I had really understood it. He was the fraud and cheat.

Now there was my mother to face. As I crept home I realized there was no need to assume that she would see me as a branded outcast. She was more likely to worry about my being entered in a dossier somewhere and that the word 'cheat' against my name would dog me for the rest of my days. She had, with some reason, views about dossiers. My best hope was that her view of what she called The System would make her furious about my treatment. System or no System, she was inclined to side with teachers when I grumbled about them.

- That Powell, he never explains properly. He mumbles out of the window and you can't hear a word so I can't do my decimals and always get the dots in the wrong place.

- You know something? Maybe he don't explain all that good or maybe someone else sometimes looks out of the window or fools around with Manny and doesn't pay attention. If I went up to the school and asked how come you don't know decimals, I might hear a thing or two wouldn't make you seem so hard done by.

- Did I say anything about going up to school? You'll make me look like a real mummy's boy. You'll make me look like a real fool.

- I don't have to try. You're making a good job of that without my help.

The matter was left there and she made it very clear that there was no future in spilling out all my little grievances. But if she sniffed out some real injustice she'd be up at the school like a shot. She had already had one or two brushes with Mr Margolis and he'd learned to treat her with care, almost deference.

- Who does he think he is? God? He can make himself a ganzer macher with little kids but as far as I'm concerned he's just a tin-pot bully. You see, he's part of The System. He has to teach you to obey, to do what you're told, no questions asked. You know why? Because that's what you're supposed to do for the rest of your life, be a stummer little tuchas-lecher. Very nice for the bosses. Don't worry, I'll have a word or two with him.

A word or two! I hugged myself. What I would have given to have heard her with a word or two, teaching Mr Margolis about The System. And then I had to remember that when it suited her turn the tin-pot bully was a stern wise man, a malamed. And then it was, 'He's got letters after his name, you know that? BSc. That's a degree from a university. It means he's a scientist. You can learn a thing or two from a man like that'.

Out tumbled my story as soon as I got home and I cried again for a bit.

- Enough, enough, she said with her arm round me. Sometimes I think he's a bit touched, screaming his head off and hitting little boys. Other times I think he just pretends to go mad like that because he thinks the kids might all run wild like little gangsters. Mind you, he'd no business to hit you with the stick just for moving your lips. It's like it was for the Jews in the Tzar's army. Hurting and hitting is no way for a school. Or, come to that, for a man who's been to college.

- What about my marks and making me bottom?
- Your marks, your marks.

She was miles away, talking to herself.

- Bottom, he's making me bottom! He's the cheat, not me!
- I'll speak to him, she said quietly. Wash your face and go make yourself a platzel and cream cheese.

She spoke to him. I got all my marks, even the arithmetic. The cane she could not take back. As for cheating, I'd begun to think about it.

When it came to it I chose to do Latin. At the beginning of the third year we all had to start on German. They gave you a short dose, three weeks with Mr Jones and *Deutches Leben* and then they asked you if you wanted to continue or do Latin instead. A choice! Every other subject in the curriculum had fallen upon us like acts of God. No one had asked at the beginning of the first year whether we fancied five years' worth of French or a similar sentence of doing chemistry with bloody-minded Mr Old. It was strictly table d'hote. Faced with this new phenomenon, choice, we could have done with a little advice. Not a word. At other schools there would have been some parents who knew about such things or thought they did. Our parents together could have mustered a lot of languages, Yiddish, Russian, Polish, Lithuanian and the men could all read Hebrew. It wouldn't have struck us that this qualified them to tell us about German and Latin. All their languages were part of their incurable immigrant backwardness, usually spoken because they couldn't speak English or couldn't speak it very well or just weren't comfortable with it. As for Hebrew which they didn't speak, they read it because that's how you practised your religion. That's how they learnt their prayers and were able to get to grips with the Torah and the Talmud. German and Latin we knew were something quite different, real languages with textbooks, declensions and conjugations and you could do them for Matric. The teachers could have said a word or two but they didn't. They certainly didn't compete for our custom. Our own folk-lore had it that lawyers and doctors needed Latin though no one seemed to know why. We knew that you didn't learn Latin so that you could go and speak it to the Latins. And Latin used to happen in the school stories we read. None of that mattered very much to me. I was plumping for Latin.

It was like this. English was the language spoken in my house. All the adults could speak Yiddish fluently but they only used it when they didn't want the children to understand or when people came to the house who were only at home in Yiddish - which was most of them. The English spoken was peppered with Yiddish words, exclamations, curses, threats, proverbs. Their English had occasional touches of Yiddish grammar and was usually spoken with a distinctive Yiddish lilt. They sang Yiddish lullabies and folk songs, 'Herrt a meisser, kindele', 'Az der rebbe Eli Meli ist geworen sehr gefreli'. I picked up a lot of Yiddish this way and would not have spoken it at all if it weren't for the fact that in the homes of all my friends Yiddish was the language you lived in. Simply to be civil, say 'please' and 'thank you', 'good Sabbath', 'Is Solly in?' I had to muster some working Yiddish. I was never really fluent with it but all my school friends could speak it as confidently as they spoke English and they usually spoke to their parents in it. There was even Manny's father who, as a Jewish socialist, was militant about Yiddish. 'Forget Hebrew', he would say, 'it's for the Zionists. Yiddish is the language of the Jewish proletariat'. As a member of the Bund he sent Manny to evening classes at the Workers' Circle where a scholarly little man introduced him to the Yiddish literary canon. Sholem Aleichem, Isaac Perets, Sholom Asch and the rest.

Neither I nor my classmates would have known that Yiddish began as a mediaeval German dialect. It was only when we began our classes that it dawned on us that German sounded very familiar. The fluent Yiddish speakers were cock-a-hoop. If only French had been like this. As Nat said, 'German's only posh Yiddish'. Whole sentences and dozens of words were understood immediately. They all took to German like ducks to water. Mr Jones couldn't go fast enough for them. But my nose was out of joint. I was floundering. It is Latin for me, I thought. At least we'll all start level pegging. So eight of us went down the corridor to the Sixth Form Library, all oak panels and glass-fronted book cabinets. We were an elite before we'd started.

Mr Chester, the Latin master, was a bit remote but quite a gentle man. With only eight of us to teach he relaxed all the disciplinary ploys. No one was given lines nor detentions, nor made the butt of sarcasms and savageries. We were a cosy little club. And Latin wasn't difficult at all. You didn't have to try to speak it. Once you had galloped through all the conjugations and declensions you translated simple little phony sentences about Lucius, the line of battle, centurions and Gaul. Then you progressed to concocted little paragraphs mostly military or mythological. At the begininning of the Fourth Year our happy little band were in for a bit of a shock. We had Virgil's *Aeneid,* Book Two, the Trojan Horse one, thrown at us and we suddenly felt we knew no Latin at all. You had to prepare a chunk at home the night before a lesson. It was slow work. The standard little blue edition of the time had a driblet of Virgil's text wedged between an Introduction and the Notes and Glossary. I pored over the pages, fluttering to and fro, in an effort to drag some kind of meaning from them. All very rabbinical. Back in the class the ancient method persisted. You took it in turns to translate a ration of lines. Latin had become a wearisome grind. Mr Chester, with no recriminations, would patiently help out if you got stuck but there was no joy in it at all.

Then the word went round that if you went to Foyles in the Charing Cross Road you could buy an English translation of Book Two, quite cheap as well.

'It's what's called a crib', Simon Frumkin said with authority. 'A crib?' I asked. 'Funny word.' 'It's a book to cheat with, schmeryl'. So we elected him our book buyer and he came back from Foyles with a clutch of these so-called cribs. I took my copy and went off to a quiet corner to examine it. I took an immediate dislike to it. It looked and felt as though it had been printed on thin blotting paper. There wasn't very much of it. The text had been crammed into almost all of the available space on the page and the print was microscopic and slightly fuzzy. Nothing broke up the unrelieved tedium of the pages. There was only the identification at the top of page one, Classical Translations No. 27, *Aeneid* Book 2, B L Braithwaite, BA. If ever you wanted to make a publication look like under-the-desk contraband, this was it. The translation was in an English which had been tortured to enable desperate learners to match phrase with phrase. My disgust did not prevent me from using it though I never took it into class out of a kind of squeamishness I didn't know I had in me. I certainly didn't want Mr Chester to catch me with anything so obviously grubby, without the slightest pretence of being a real book and manifestly designed as a swindle. I mustn't overdo my distaste, though. That crib saved me hours and hours of slavery. High-minded principles were not going to stand in my way.

Then one day I was in Whitechapel Library. It was one of those magnificent Carnegie libraries which the old London Boroughs prided themselves on. Its stock was as good as a university for many people in the East End. I didn't know my way around the shelves all that well. I usually headed for the novels and, less often, a book to help me with my homework. Tentatively, I had picked up *All Quiet on the Western Front* and *Brave New World* which an English teacher had suggested and I'd toyed with Trevelyan's *History* but, glancing at a few pages, I could see it was over my head. I was wandering past some unfamiliar shelves when I spotted a large handsome collection of many books. I could see there were really two collections in the same format, one bound in green and the other in red. I went closer and read their titles. Here, I realized, were the classics, all of them, Greek in green, Latin in red. I looked along the Latin shelves and there was Virgil's *Aeneid*. I loved the feel and look of it, good paper and friendly type-face. It had class. I saw it as coming from a world where fastidious gentlemen sat in leather armchairs and read it easily and earnestly. Flicking through the pages, I realized there was something unusual about the book. I had no idea such books existed. On the right-hand page there was the Latin text and on the left an English translation. I hunted for Book Two and for the bit I had just been working on, Anchises being carried from burning Troy. The translator, I could see even then, had been free and easy, making his prose read like a real English book. I stood and read a page or two, savouring it. I had stumbled on the Loeb Classics.

I took the book out and went home. I flung Braithwaite into a corner, planning from then on to work only with my find. I wish I could say that I was a really generous-minded youth and immediately shared my find with the other founder members of the Latin club. I didn't let the thought cross my mind. It was my own discovery and besides, they were satisfied with their grimy cribs. They'd find out soon enough anyway because I was going to take my treasure quite openly to the Latin class. Mr Chester, I was sure, would be pleased and perhaps impressed.

It came my turn to translate. I took my book from my satchel, placed it on the desk and began glancing from time to time at it and my own notebook. I had scarcely translated two lines when Mr Chester stopped me.

- Rosen, what have you got there? He sounded quite surprised.

- A translation I have been using, sir, I said chirpily.

Mr Chester was looking genuinely baffled and, I thought, a little hurt.

- You know that's a crib. You not only bring a crib into class but you open it under my very nose. Don't you think that's a bit silly?

- But, sir, this isn't a crib. This is a Loeb Classic.

I said 'Loeb Classic' as others might have talked of the Seven Wonders of the World. Mr Chester smiled and nearly laughed.

- Rosen, if you bring a Loeb Classic to class it becomes a crib. There's no difference at all.

He picked up my book and read a bit to himself.

- Fine translation. Don't bring it to class again, there's a good lad.

The club members bunched round me after class. They weren't angry or jealous. They just wanted to thumb the book and enjoy it a bit. After that they always came to me to copy out the next passage. But I felt cheated.

Whenever I went past the Mission to the Jews in Philpot street I thought of Gothic. I mean the Gothic language. I first encountered Gothic as soon as I went to the University. Like most people I had never heard of it before and I've heard almost nothing of it ever since. It doesn't exactly crop up. Somebody had decided that if you were to get a degree in English Language and Literature then you simply had to study Gothic. On the face of it the connection between the two was not too obvious to an eighteen-year-old. I suppose that tucked away in some dusty archive in the Senate House there is a solemn rationale for this bizarre element in our course. The main thing is that Gothic is the earliest Germanic language known to the trade and no doubt there were scholars who got very excited about this. It's a bit like those people who get quite a buzz out of tracing their ancestors back to the Normans. Perhaps there was a lot more to it than that but I had expected university English to be one long round of delight and professors talking like Quiller Couch and Leslie Stephen and endless days reading novels and poems and plays. But here on my timetable was Gothic (to say nothing of Anglo-Saxon, Phonetics and Palaeography) on Monday mornings at 10 a.m. with Dr Brookfield.

I had been far too naive to investigate beforehand what English actually meant at university, and when I discovered it meant Gothic, that was a nasty shock. I went off to buy my Gothic textbook in a rebellious frame of mind. Page after disheartening page of Gothic grammar which I discovered very soon was mostly invented on the basis of some identikit principles which I never fully understood. The grammar book had asterisks against the word forms they had made up. Most of the words had asterisks against them. I took it to the first class with Dr Brookfield. She was a frail-looking oldish lady with a chalky white face and wire-wool hair. She always wore a navy-blue dress with a white lace collar and round her neck was a large ornate gold cross. We soon found that she was an amiable lady though as a mentor she might have been made of steel. I remember that in her first hour with us she told us we were going to study a Gothic text by someone with the unlikely name of Ulfilas. We'd find it at the back of our text book. This Ulfilas had translated the Bible into Gothic in the fourth century AD. It turned out that only a few tiny bits and pieces of Ulfilas's mighty work had survived and some of this is what we had to prepare for translation in class. So this was going to be our dry bread and water for the year and the price we had to pay for enjoying ourselves with Chaucer and Shakespeare was a fictional grammar and old scraps of the Bible in an utterly outlandish language.

Then Dr Brookfield suggested that we should all toddle off to the British Museum just down the road to take a look at Franks Casket. That had a nice homely ring. It turned out to be a decorated box with runic inscriptions all round it. We didn't know why Dr Brookfield had told us to go and look at it. Maybe Mr Ulfilas wrote in runes. Were there quotes from him on it? Was it a casket from Gothic times made in Gothic-land? Why was it called Franks Casket? Was it made by Frank or for the Franks? I found in a corner of the display case a puzzling translation of the runes and enjoyed an indecisive bit which read, 'The whale became sad (or, The ocean became turbid)'. The scholars didn't seem too sure about their precious Gothic. After all, there's quite a difference between an ocean and a whale. Dr Brookfield never mentioned Franks Casket again. She might just as well have sent us to look at the Rosetta Stone. Perhaps she knew how baffled and dismayed we were by the prospect of the Monday Gothic hour and thought a pretty little ivory casket with carvings of the Adoration of the Magi and Wayland the Smith on it might cheer us up. Doesn't seem likely. After I'd been in the college a few months I'd got to know the very popular beadle in the cloisters in his claret frock coat and gold-braided topper. His name was Frank. I said one day.

- You know, Frank, your name's in the British Museum. They've named a box after you.

- Have they now? A student told me that when I came here in 1928 and I said, 'Listen, Sonny Jim, Frank's a very common name but you can keep your comic turns for your clever pals' I may be wearing a funny hat but I'm not a museum piece yet.

Back in our class we were soon on the treadmill, preparing and translating the fragments of Ulfilas. The first year English group, it must be said, consisted mostly of young women who came in from the outer suburbs each day. They were clever, very diligent and almost always unquestioning. Ulfilas was not their favourite writer. They didn't think he was a good read any more than I did. He'd given them a nasty surprise, too. But they sighed and got down to it, arriving in class with their tidy files and flawless handwriting. If you had to do Gothic to get a degree in English, so be it. They were not ones for teach-ins, sit-ins, picket lines, boycotts and protests. That came much later. Most of them were very up-front Christians and that turned out to be important for me. The bits of Gothic we had to translate were from the New Testament. I recollect that one was that passage about 'where moth doth corrupt and thieves break in and steal'. Another was the Lord's Prayer.

I had never read the New Testament. The very idea of reading it was distasteful to me. This was not a religious objection. I wasn't religious. I didn't go to synagogue except to keep my grandfather company on the few occasions when he went as an act of solidarity. My scant, rote-learnt Hebrew was disappearing fast. No, getting into the New Testament would be like going over to the other side, kissing its icons. The name Jesus I found difficult to say. He was their Man, not mine. My Christian classmates, of course, were not finding translation the least bit difficult, if you can call it translation. They scarcely had to look at the Gothic - they knew that stuff by heart. I ask you, the Lord's Prayer! At eighteen I might have heard of it but I certainly didn't know it.

Gif uns himma daga ....

Give us this day ....

Perhaps Dr Brookfield knew why I was having difficulty, or partly knew. If she did she gave not the slightest indication. But then, none of the lecturers ever gave a flicker of awareness that *The Jew of Malta* or *The Merchant of Venice* or *The Prioresse's Tale* might be making me resentfully uncomfortable. We were doing literature, not politics. And, as someone once said, maybe English is not a university subject for Jews.

So it was that I seethed in the first few classes and spent far too many hours preparing bloody Ulfilas while the young women could spare time mugging up Germanic sound changes, the Great Vowel Shift, Grimm's Law, Verner's Law. One of them said to me one day

- You're a funny chap, Rosen, you really are. All you've got to do is buy yourself a copy of the New Testament. And then she added wickedly, still, you might lose a grievance that way.

She was right. I had to get a New Testament. If translating bits of it was a kind of betrayal, imagine what a total defection buying it would be, actually walking into a shop and buying one. This was to give a home to their Book on my shelves. To hear coming out of it their words. Buy it I couldn't. Remember, no one had ever said to me that I mustn't read that book. I don't think they ever referred to it. They banned it by silence. Yet I knew how shocked they would be if they knew that my course obliged me to buy it and read it. I exaggerate, there were some people at home who would not have turned a hair and maybe even laughed. My Uncle Sam might have said, 'Comparative Religion, eh? Very advanced!'

I could go so far and no further. I was not going to buy it. Borrow one from the library maybe? Copy out chunks before returning it? Tedious. Suddenly the solution came to me and I laughed to myself at the beauty of the irony. The Mission to the Jews.

Philpot Street Synagogue was a large building disguised as a Greek temple with its fat columns and pediment. A few buildings further along the road was the Mission to the Jews. When I was young this seemed to me like a most wilful act of provocation but when I was a teenager a couple of friends and I found the Mission very funny and also enigmatic. We could not imagine any adult we knew ever going into the place. What for? What would they say? 'Good morning, I'd like to be a Christian. How long does it take, please? Does it cost?' Manny said,

- You ever heard of a Jew becoming a Christian? You couldn't make yourself into a goy even if you wanted to. You couldn't talk like one, you couldn't eat like one, you couldn't look like one.

- Henriques talks like one and looks like one.

- Oh, him. He's Sephardic, that's different. Even so, he hasn't become a Christian. He takes Jewish prayers in that boys' club of his.

- So you tell me. That building over there. Must cost a fortune. They do it all for nothing?

We were sitting on a low wall opposite the mission. It was about five o'clock and we'd decided to settle a problem. We'd never seen anyone going in or out, would-be convert or missionary. Who were they, these missionaries? What did they look like? How many were there? We soon found out. At their closing time, four of them came out of the front door, three men and a woman. They all wore sober clothes which we thought of as gentile and seemed to us, though I think we invented it, downcast and furtive. They certainly weren't sprightly in their step nor did they look round with good cheer. Manny said,

- And that lot think they're going to make us all Christians?

Some hopes.

- Nice job, though, being a Jew-converter. You don't lift a finger, year in, year out, and get paid for it.

- You know, there's a woman in Varden Street married into a Jewish family. A shiksa she is - well, was - but she converted. Learnt all the prayers and everything. And what about Rutman's presser? Speaks Yiddish better than me and he's a goy. Old Rutman thinks it's marvellous. He keeps saying to him for a joke, 'Henry, you speak Yiddish so good you should get circumcised'.

- That's all different, said Manny. There's no Mission to the Christians, is there? And there'd be a right shemozzle if there was. It's different, isn't it? He didn't sound all that sure.

And now, just because of Ulfilas I was on my way to this same Mission to the Jews. The beauty of it was that I wasn't swallowing my pride and giving in to the quiet tyranny of old Ulfilas. I was going to put one over him. I pushed open the door and there in the large hall was a desk, all very neat. There were small stacks of pamphlets and a letter rack. Around the hall were posters with quotable bits of the New Testament in large black letters. And there were some in Hebrew. I hadn't expected that. I had expected lots of pictures of Jesus Christ extending his arms over little children with blond curls. Or the Crucifix. Of them not a sign. A man behind the desk looked up when I came in. I told myself that he was amazed. I had prepared my great chutzpah performance.

- Do sit down. Can I help?

- Yes, I said firmly. I have never read the New Testament, you see, and I'd very much like to do so.

The man brightened up.

- Do you think I could borrow one for a short while?

- Borrow one? We'd be happy to give you one.

He pulled open a drawer and with a touch of ceremony handed me a New Testament. I have it to this very day. Soft black leather covers extending beyond the body of the book and fine rice paper made it flexible and different. I got up to go. But he wasn't going to let this occasion slip by so easily.

- Would you mind waiting just a moment? I'd like you to meet our Director.

He edged me into a nearby room. I hadn't bargained for this. The Director, a man with a gold watch chain across a black waistcoat, in no time was asking me questions. Was I a student?

Why did I want to read the New Testament? Would I like to know more about Christianity? Would I like to meet a group of Christian students? I improvised feebly, almost always with a lie. When they asked for my name and address ('to keep in touch') I invented them. They pressed pamphlets on me. I fled from the place, knowing things hadn't turned out to be such a laugh after all. But I had my New Testament and when I next saw Manny I gave him a full report. 'I missed being baptised by a whisker'.

I was still sufficiently aggrieved about the Ulfilas business to be determined to be quite open with my New Testament. I went into class, smiled at the others and spread it out at the right page. When my turn came I consulted it with slow deliberation. Dr Brookfield drew up alongside me.

- Mr Rosen, she said as quietly as ever, have you prepared this passage?

- Most carefully, Dr Brookfield.

- In that case, why do you need this crib?

She lifted the New Testament, rather irreverently, I thought. By now I was sick of the childishness of it all.

- No, Dr Brookfield, this is not a crib, as you call it. This is your New Testament.

She was taken aback and I instantly regretted my improvised rudeness and wished I could withdraw it.

- Well, she said, in this class my New Testament is, I am afraid, a crib and using it is not fair to the others.

- No, I said, can't you see that the whole of this class is unfair to me?

I closed my books, stood up, stumbled along the row and left the room.

Not Yet

Detention. Just six of us; the usual crimes, the usual criminals - me, Solly, Berko, Saxy, Mo (of course) and the unknown quantity, Hoffman. The crime sheet was so routine you could have run it off for the whole term on the old Gestetner. Talking in class, calling out, passing notes, homework not in on time, lying - conduct prejudicial to good order and discipline. All down in Brock's flawless hand. So flawless, so durable and ineradicable, it turned our follies and foibles into everlasting wickedness so that we despaired of ever going straight. But Hoffman was new, only two months with us, His clothes were more expensive than ours, dapper men's, not youth's, shoes and silk shirts, I do believe. He was more pink than us, his hair was straight and fine and sandy. He was more suave too. We thought him, I hesitate, almost - well, Gentile. He was in for cheek rather than chutzpah. To Gobby with whom we had long since learned not to trifle. Gobby had been pursuing an earnest enquiry about nouns in apposition and drawn Hoffman into the quest. 'I've never been taught that - er, Sir.' Harmless enough, but this Hoffman could languidly imply that, if he hadn't been taught such things, they weren't worth knowing or at any rate he shouldn't be pestered about them. Gobby did his eye-flicker for a second or so and then struck, as we knew he would. He was suddenly affable even solicitous. - Ah yes. It has crossed my mind that your last school left you a little-er-unfinished. We can help a little. May I suggest you present yourself in Room 23 at 4 o'clock?

Hoffman tried to get out a word ....

- No need to thank me. You'll find it all works out best if

you arrive strictly on time. Now take this example, 'Albert, the Prince Regent ....' And we were back on course. Meanwhile Hoffman had smiled gratefully at the unlooked for chance to study the detention system.

So here he was with the old lags looking less cast down and aggrieved than us and less tousled by the wear and tear of a school day. No ink on his hands, tie and collar fit for a studio photograph, no marks of brawling or chesting a wet football. We mooched to the empty desks, sullen and grumpy but resigned, dumped ourselves down and dropped our satchels on the floor. We spread ourselves around like strangers, knowing if we didn't we'd only be separated in a minute or two. Hoffman hadn't moved yet. He slowly gave the whole room the once over, his inspection drifting past us. He made his fastidious choice and sauntered over to the desk nearest to the door under the baize notice-board, next to the fire-extinguisher. We watched him and his almost adult ways. Not our kind of adults though. Ours overfilled their clothes and spilled schmalz on them, they walked with their feet close to the ground, toes outwards, heads bent forward and turned towards each other, and they poked fingers into each other's shoulders. They were cocooned in communal noise, did not know about Private Persons. They all talked at once, shouted as they slapped down their dominoes at the Workers' Circle or slurped their lemon tea or bitterly cursed the tailoring trade in noisy knots at the corner of Great Garden Street. No, what the adult Hoffman was shaping up for was more like those occasional figures you saw stalking down the Whitechapel Road who came from Outside and made your mind shuffle uneasily at the faint whiff of power they gave off. They dealt with others, haunted offices or inspected something and never looked to right or left to catch sight of a relative or someone from the same stettel back in the East. Up there in the Sixth Form where they put on white coats to do Zoology there were one or two who were beginning to get the knack and might soon pass themselves off as the real thing. Golly Gottlieb came to school with a rolled umbrella and he was going to study at the London School of Economics, whatever that was. Gluckstein, whose father owned the big furniture shop opposite the Jewish Reading Room, had taken to wearing a fine light grey suit which clearly had not come out of the tailoring dens off the Commercial Road. A lawyer he was going to be and he had already closed his face to get into that part. Had they stopped eating pickled herring and latkes? Maybe you could learn how to do it. But then they couldn't have been the sort who had landed up regularly in detention when they were in the third year. Hoffman's kind of adult we saw in the pictures at the Rivoli or Palaseum, poised possessors of occasions, velvet public movers, who knew how to stand, walk or confer the benefit of themselves on a chair, always affable but always inviolable. But this Hoffman wasn't out of a film and was no Sixth Former. New he might be, but his lot was cast in with ours, a Third Former with an essay to do on Henry IV Part One, trying to get the hang of simultaneous equations, chanting defective Latin verbs for next Friday's test, listening to forty minutes uninterrupted droning on the Factory Acts and scribbling the notes from the board. What's more we'd noticed he wasn't too good at that kind of thing. As if that mattered. For the moment we were not competing furtively for B pluses and As but studying his glide over to the desk by the fire extinguisher and his so English manner of gracing the seat. It was already said by the know-all yuchners that he'd never been to cheder classes and, though this was beyond belief, that he'd not been barmitzvah-ed. Was that how you did it and got to be a Sixth Former before your time?

So we sat and endured the minutes. Mo was gently rattling coins in his pockets, Solly was drawing on the little pad he carried around, Saxy was whistling pianissimo through his teeth and drawn back lips, Berko cheated of his football was torturing himself by listening to the sound of the ball being thumped about outside. I was looking at Hoffman. He was leaning back in his seat and waiting, it seemed from the beginnings of a rosy smile, for a performance to begin.

If anything stirred beneath our torpor it was speculation about who would be the master in charge of this detention. And it mattered. If it was going to be Burroughs, he would give out dictionaries, select an arbitrary page and you copied out entries for an hour. 'Wouldn't want to be wasting your precious time', he would say. Leggy would make us sit in total silence, arms folded, eyes front. (All of them had been in the army). Then he'd read his paper or savagely mark books. He once crossed out a page of my futile maths with such ferocity that his red pencil slashed the page open. He had to be watched, for he had a filthy temper and we had just enough prudence to be wary of him. In detentions he would glance up often enough to take a good shufti at us and spot a backslider who would be made to stand facing the wall with his nose touching it. O'Shea on the other hand made it clear that he was bored out of his mind himself and he just used to chat with us and encourage us to be ever so slightly cheeky.

- Where d'you buy suits like that? We'd ask about his rural peatbrown Harris tweed the like of which we'd never clapped eyes on.

- Buy 'em? You don't buy 'em. They get handed down as heirlooms.

- Did you really play hockey for your university?

- Yes, he'd say, we didn't win a ghost of a match that year. And don't be prying so much.

- Which football team do you support?

- And why should I be supporting a football team? Haven't I got my work cut out supporting meself and me aged mother? I won't be taking on a football team till I'm a Headmaster and mebbe even then, the money won't run to it

We had just begun to detect the Celtic fringe amongst our teachers and had a dim and wildly inaccurate notion of what it all amounted to. But a kind of humour came into it somewhere and anyway O'Shea was good value, especially in the deserts of detentions. Imagine trying to talk to Gobby like that. No, that would be like trying to imagine him with his trousers down or doing a Highland fling. When Gobby took detention you stayed on the alert every second. No Yiddish obscenities and curses meant to be just heard but not understood, no deaf-and-dumb signals across the spaces, no scamping of chores, no ostentatious shufflings and coughings, no slumping from mock exhaustion as the clock dragged towards five, no cross-legged squirmings and asking to be excused and staying for five minutes to watch the football. No nothings with Gobby. You could forget the whole repertoire of diversions from tedium and illicit resistances. Gobby never raised his voice, never gave a sign of teacherly outrage or distress, just that sinister flicker of the eyelids, a slight pursing of the lips, a sniff or two, the handkerchief drawn from the sleeve, dab, dab, then a stiletto sentence. With him it was all heads down and not a whimper of rebellion.

It turned out in a minute or two that it was Mr King's stint for the detention shift. We called him Queenie not just to turn the world verbally upside down nor even because we saw him as a homosexual. We knew neither the word nor the idea. It was just that he moved talked and engaged with us in ways we knew only from women. Even his public school speech was the soft caressing variety you hear in some artists and writers - all the same sounds but articulated in a different place and with a different music coaxed out of them. Poor old Queenie! He might just as well have presented his jugular to ravening wolves as come amongst us with his alien kind of chivalry, gentleness and vulnerability, his inability to disguise his hurt at rejection and mockery. Easy enough to recognise years later that there was a man it would have been good to know and learn from, but then he was nothing more than a perfect prey, a goy with a difference. He belonged to that little band of folk who are not made for this wicked world, should not be let out alone. They must be protected, taken round ambushes, have their tickets bought for them and be put on trains while they are freed to go on thinking about Baudelaire. He was certainly no person to send into the lair of Yiddisher knuckers, coarse clever-dicks ever on the look-out for a rare sacrificial victim. We'd never run into his like, someone both clever and easily wounded, articulate but without a repertoire of put-downs, humiliated but not a humiliator, knowledgeable about books but not about boys. Poor fellow, he paid for it all. We sacrificed him without remorse. Such a schmeryl! Strange revenges for our own hurts which we could not have put in words flowed against him. Without personal animosity we demolished him and scored it up as a little victory, against all the nameless defeats. What a misfortune to be a nice man without a shell amongst such frustrated predators.

Queenie came bouncing into the room with all the simulated energy of the fearful. Insubordination flickered into life immediately and Queenie was saying through the escalating disorder. 'Now, look chaps. Do something sensible, eh. You can start on your homework. It'll save you time later. Read a book. The hour will go more quickly. Or why don't you . . .' We orchestrated a huge clatter with our satchels, complained about empty ink-wells, chuntered to each other mimicking and mocking his speech, turning it into foppish silliness. We half-began a bit of reading or set about an exercise. Queenie teetered on the edge of total impotence and we teetered on the edge of open defiance and worse. I do not like to think about it now. It's not only a squeamish recoil from the cruelties. Nor is it that a mere eight years later I was on the receiving end, having gone over to the enemy. It is because I know now why we were pitted against one another in the detention room and that poor Queenie could never have known where it had all gone wrong for him. He had his first class French degree (Cantab.) and a gown. Why had he been set down amongst these pitiless torturers, with their outlandish names and outlandish noises?

We were all in it except Hoffman. He was eye-ing Queenie in his long black gown, and was leaning back in his seat, not joining in with the rest of us, just steadily watching the fluttering and flappings of the wounded bird - in a nicely restrained sort of way, a well-balanced spectator in the better part of the house.

We simmered and simmered towards five o'clock. If it had been the whole class, we would have erupted but a scattered handful we kept an eye on the boundaries. Solly's thumb and forefinger had a frozen hold on the top of a page of a textbook. Berko had written a few scratchy lines in an exercise book. If Queenie's glance lighted on him, he advertised himself as someone grappling with difficult ideas. In between foghorn yawns Saxy was fiddling with his maths homework. He loved the damn stuff really. And Mo was keeping up a grumbling mutter, looking up occasionally to the ceiling with his eyes shut and then down to an open book: this was his regular learning-something-by-heart performance. Oh yes. We each had our little fail-safe system on the go. We didn't overdo it. The work was at best sporadic but just enough. Between whiles there was a good laugh. Berko could belch at will and control the volume and texture to suit the occasion or his fancy. He chose his moments to crackle and rumble knowing his virtuosity and variety always had us in fits.

- Ach, such a filthy chuzza! We applauded.

The rule book laid down the iron laws of a well-run detention but some teachers worked their own little variations. If you were in luck, at about half-time, they'd leave you to it and nip up to the staff room. A teacher would look round at the class, assure himself we were moderately cowed, walk up and down the rows a couple of times to uncover any illicit goings-on. (A comic, I remember, was a very illicit going-on or any kind of sweet-popping). Then he'd make slowly for the door and turn for a last quelling stare. We'd glisten with good behaviour and pray. And he'd be gone. A calculated brief silence just in case. And then . . .

- All right for him. I'm busting for a piss
- Gone for a quick drag
- A quick drag! With that pipe. It'll take him till five to get it going
- Doing his betting slips
- Chaim Schmerl went to the races
  Lost his gutgas and his braces . . .
- Such a voice! A chazan we should make of him

Then we'd shush each other up and drop to whispers while the detention master took his ease in the Staff Room. None of us had ever been into that secret lair. At most you got a glimpse of billowing tobacco smoke, dusty tomes, tatty old leather armchairs, huge heaps of grimy exercise books and a flickering coal fire. Where else in the world could there be a room like it? Gobby once sent me up to get Funk and Wagnell's Dictionary on a dull winter's evening. The gaunt joyless Brock stood in the doorway without his gown, the keeper of Hell's Gate. Behind him I caught a glimpse of the other masters floating eerily in the smoke touched by the light of the fire. They seemed dead and doomed.

No point in Queenie waiting for a lull. He took his chance, left us to our bogus work and bolted out of the door.

Hoffman said, it's 4.27, and crossed off another minute in his Rough Work Book. Then he swung his legs out from under the desk and stretched them out over the top. There were sharp creases in his trousers. Berko moved to the window to watch the footballers who were doing without him. Someone behind me was patiently picking a hole in the thick oak desk top with his geometry compass. Suddenly Hoffman said in a loud voice, how does this thing work? He was lightly tapping the fire-extinguisher above his head. It didn't sound like a serious question All the same we all turned towards him. Berko turned his head from the window and the woodpecker behind me stopped tap-tapping.

- Tells you on the side.

The fire-extinguisher we all knew. Amongst all the battered wood, splintered parquet, scratched brown varnish, pockmarked tiles and flaking distemper its gorgeous red, black and gold looked like a mistake. In every classroom they were untouched and untouchable. We'd all read the instructions 'In case of fire . . .' and so forth. Please God, we'd never need to use it. Enough trouble without emergencies. Emergency exits; in emergency use hammer to break windows; the coiled hose; life-belts; high voltage; electrified rails, do not cross the lines. Emergencies we could do without.

- Don't you know then? said Hoffman.

Mo couldn't resist.

- There's a sort of hammer fixed to the side. And there's that pin. Stops you moving the hammer. When you pull the pin out, you can move the hammer up and down. You just lift the hammer up and bash it down on the side and that .... Mo stopped as he realized Hoffman was listening seriously and taking note.

But Hoffman said, That sounds really stupid. Don't believe a word of it, Pins and hammers. You don't expect me to swallow that, do you?

- He's meshiggah, Solly whispered to me. We were uneasy. We had our sense of things getting out of hand.

Hoffman was on his feet. A panicky voice said, Leave it, Hoffman. But Hoffman already had the pin out and was looking contemptuously at us. He lifted the hammer and let it drop onto the side of the extinguisher. Clonk! Nothing happened.

- You see? said Hoffman, you're so stupid. It doesn't work like that.

We were getting desperate. Little wickednesses were one thing but sin on this scale was beyond us. There would be some terrible retribution. Grand audacity was for others.

- You're right, you're right, we told him. Only leave the bloody thing alone. You'll damage it. Just leave it alone, leave it alone.

Hoffman fingered the hammer again. We were squeaking with cowardly anxiety.

- We'll all cop it. God knows what they'll do to us.

Hoffman found our performance distasteful. Swiftly he turned his back on us, lifted the hammer and smashed it down against the fire extinguisher. White foam came gushing out of the nozzle and hit the front of the classroom, a gorgeous white froth, unstoppable and wondrous. We fell into a bewitched silence. Hoffman grabbed the thing from the wall and sprayed it nonchantly about, having the time of his life.

- Should be put away, the schmendrik. Certified -

- Locked-up.

We palpitated with shock and delight. The foam began to spread over the floor, over the desks and around our feet. It was irresistible. We started kicking it about, romping in it, shouting with abandon. White flecks spattered on trousers and jackets.

- Get it out of here! Shove it in the corridor! Stick it in the book cupboard!

We hoped he wouldn't. Hoffman's posture had become heroic. He pointed the nozzle like a fixed bayonet. He would hold out till the last round. There should have been a camera.

The foam still gushed. Somewhere beyond our jolly paddling and splashing a nerve of panic still throbbed.

- Get Queenie, Saxy said. We laughed our heads off at such a delicious possibility. Queenie in this madhouse. Saxy wasn't joking. He paddled out of the room and was back in no time with a flushed Queenie struggling to look masterful and cool. He was on the edge of tears. He rushed madly at Hero Hoffman to grab the extinguisher. Hoffman somehow didn't time his release too well. By the time Queenie was in full-possession after the badly-managed transfer there were gobbets of foam down the front of Queenie's suit. He steadied himself and adjusted his grip while the extinguisher sprayed around wildly. We faked terror, ducking and side-stepping.

Queenie shouted, Open a window, open a window. That one.

Two of us wrestled for the window pole. The winner waved it around the catch, found it and tugged. We egged him on, choking on our laughter. And while the foam still sprayed Queenie hopped up and down with the fire extinguisher as though he were holding a bomb. He wanted none of it, having no taste for emergencies himself. His face was bright red and creased with anxiety.

At last the window squeaked open and Queenie rushed up to it. With his only touch of masterly control he directed the nozzle out of the window. At his first go the jet hit a window pane but he adjusted his aim and got on target. The creases dropped from his face. But at the very moment of his triumph the stream of foam curled into a weak arc. Queenie stood his ground as though hoping for better things. And then a last feeble dribble splashed onto the floor. Queenie's shoulders dropped and he let the extinguisher hang from his hands.

To a man we burst into cheers and jumped up and down beside ourselves. All caution gone we let rip, mounting a huge din.

- You silly, silly man, I heard Hoffman saying while clapping appreciatively.

Suddenly, Queenie turned on us hugging the gleaming red extinguisher, his legs apart. Yes, I was sure now, his eyes were brimming with tears. The cheers died slowly into a silence. Queenie came a step nearer. Out of his anguish he yelled.

What do you people come here for? What do you want of us?

As if we knew. Perhaps Hoffman did. But we didn't. Not for sure. Not yet.

Penmanship

All Mr O'Carroll's teaching of writing skills rested on the one foundation principle - 'Up thin, down thick'. He was a methodical man and as a writing master his procedure was unvarying. He walked up and down the rows, cane in hand to achieve a classful of impeccable calligraphers who no longer made aitches without loops, zeds and kays without their twiddly bits or mutated their Qs into gees. He walked up and down the rows, cane in hand and if you malformed a letter you put out your hand and got a stinger, delivered without mercy or malice. Up and down he went, swishing away for half an hour. This reign of terror may have worked well for some but it made my pen falter and the faint chance I had of turning out a page without blots and exotic shapes for letters vanished in my despair and resignation. Resigned I certainly was. On the day when I could see that my kay, the old enemy, had gone astray again, Mr O'Carroll was right over the other side of the room dispassionately dispensing just deserts. I realised I'd have a long wait before he got round to me. I put up my hand.

- Please, sir, my kay, I've done my kay wrong. Can I have the cane now?

Mr O'Carroll obliged and, crossing the room, delivered a whack and coolly went back to where he had left off. Give him his due, he always caned the left hand. So I tucked my hand under my arm and took up again the deformed writer's crouch. I'm afraid Mr O'Carroll put the final touches on the making of an illegible handwriter and was the cause later on of all those infuriated teachers' cries of 'I'm not even going to try to read this scribble' and 'Fit for the waste-paper basket' and those sneery remarks at the bottom of my written work in the grammar school. 'This may be the work of a genius but no one will ever know.' I couldn't very well explain to them that it was all Mr O'Carroll's fault and about that cane doing overtime and up-thin-and-down-thick.

I had one last chance to reform and, who knows, to produce manuscripts I could feel good about instead of being embarrassed by their sheer ugliness. Much of my disgruntlement was due to the fact that my scrawl was exposed day after day to my teachers' grimaces. My classmates would take a peek, too.

- Didn't know you could write Yiddish.

- A doctor, that's what you're going to be. You've got the writing for it.

- It's a code, a secret code.

I had this last chance, as I said, when I started in the grammar school. I knew we were going to do prestigious and snobby things like French, Latin and Physics, and go to a proper sports field and have a cap badge with a galleon and French motto on it, Tel grain, Tel pain. We were the elect, swept up into a rarefied air, laced with the scent of privilege. Then came a terrible blow that brought us down to earth. They told us we would be having a handwriting class. We were incredulous, insulted, humiliated. Kids' stuff. The ones whose penmanship was already as good as any adult's and whose hands raced and looped lightly across the page were sure it couldn't mean what it said. It was bound to be some kind of special writing.

- Special writing, someone said, like you see on parchment. You do it with a feather pen. Lawyers have to do it.

- It's like the way they write the Torah scrolls. You have to do it perfect. You have to do it perfect.

- That's more what you call lettering, not handwriting. They said handwriting, not lettering.

Though I joined in the outrage at being demoted in this way I secretly thought that there was just a chance that I might redeem myself and learn to write decently. So I hoped they were wrong about lettering, parchment and all that. They should be so lucky.

When the time came we were all taken by surprise. The teacher gave out something he called copybooks. We had never seen such things before. In fact even at that time most people would have regarded them as museum pieces. They looked like ordinary exercise books but they had 'Copybooks' printed on the cover and when you opened them you discovered that on each page there were printed in faultless copperplate four or five sentences like Procrastination is the thief of Time, Cleanliness is next to Godliness, The child is father to the man, Necessity is the mother of invention. Underneath each of these improving sentiments there were three lines, just like on our millboards in Miss Campbell's class when we were babies. We were expected to produce perfect replicas of the copperplate models. The class set to work, fizzing with resentment.

- If my poppa saw me doing this he'd have a fit, said Barney. He thinks we spend all day showing how clever we are like yeshiva bochers.

- Not my dad. Know what he'd say? 'So what's wrong with learning to write nice? Those people know what they're doing, I'm telling you. A degree every one of them's got. Nothing wrong with learning to write like a mensch.'

I don't know how a mensch writes but it was soon clear to me that even with the severe guidance of the model lines of copperplate my writing wasn't going to get any better. When we finally parted with the copybooks at the end of the term, everyone, myself included, reverted to the style they'd been using for years. No one's looked like copperplate. Not one of our teachers had handwriting that was faintly like copperplate. They made no comment about all this and the copybook exercise was treated as a ritual, the origin of which had been forgotten but which was kept up for good form's sake.

Between the First Year and the Fifth Year my writing got worse and worse, partly because we spent so many hours scribbling notes from the board and partly because I was always rushing my homework in the hope of leaving time to join the boys in the street. Mr Gunn, the History teacher, wrote quite beautifully on the board and very fast, too. If you didn't keep up with him he was wiping it off and starting on the next bit. Lazy Mr Powell sat on his desk, swinging his legs, fingering his little moustache and dictating at a speed nobody could keep up with. Too fast, too fast, some of us would shout. It made no difference. He swept on, caring no more about our protests than he cared about the geography he was supposed to be teaching. We prayed for a break when he would draw a map on the board, a diagrammatic one on which we could not distinguish between land and sea, rivers and boundaries. I decided in the end that the reason he'd taken to dictation was that his writing, too, was quite illegible. I had seen a page in the notebook he was dictating from when I went to the front to use the pencil sharpener. That didn't stop him crossing out my homework and writing, 'Hasty, sloppy and unreadable. Re-write. See me.' I saw him alright, at the end of the day. He'd obviously forgotten what it was all about.

- My work, I said. The Amazon. You said I've got to re-write it.

- Got it with you? No? I might have guessed. I remember now. Well, I'm not having it, my boy. Do you really expect me to spend hours and hours trying to read your stuff?

- No, sir.

- Well, I can tell you this much. Anything you write in the exam which looks like your usual mess will not be marked. You'll get nought. Get this into your noddle. The examiners are told that they're not obliged to read your kind of writing. You'll get nought. The thing is that your writing - I mean it's so uneducated - not a peasant, are you?

So he got The Amazon 'in best' as we used to say. Usually anything Mr Powell said didn't leave a lasting impression on me but we were getting very close to the matric exams. In addition to the anxieties we all shared - do I know enough to pass? - I was now alarmed at the possibility that the examiners would not even read my work. Our teachers often invoked the examiners who gradually grew in our thoughts to become implacable, omniscient ogres who wouldn't give a second thought to brushing pages of desperate work into the waste paper basket. They would settle my hash at a glance. I was very rattled. The shadows of the ever-punitive examiners darkened my frenetic revision. Abe, who was revising with me in the evenings, lost his patience.

- Why do you let a pisher like Powell put the wind up you? Er weist fon der hant und der fis. He doesn't know his arse from his elbow. Did you ever get nought for the end of year exams? For the mock exams? So leave off grizzling, will you?

I remained inconsolable.

It takes some believing but only a month or two earlier my writing had been in demand. I wrote loveletters for a sailor. I was in the Reading Room of the Whitechapel Library where some of us used to do our homework. A wiry little chap slid into the seat next to me and started muttering something or other. Eventually it turned out that he was a sailor whose ship had docked somewhere in the Thames nearby and that he needed to write to his beloved in Liverpool. He pushed a cheap little writing pad under my nose and asked me to do the job for him. It was obvious to me that he couldn't write but at first I assumed he'd dictate in whispers and I would simply be his scribe. (Me, his scribe!) But no, he wanted me to compose as well and it had to be a loveletter. Somehow he made all this clear. I don't remember what I wrote though I could make a good guess. I'd not yet written any loveletters myself but I had read a lot of novels and with shameless confidence I wrote a nice devoted piece to Agnes in Liverpool. My sailor watched my writing flowing out of my pen as though I were performing magic. He couldn't take his eyes off it. I whispered my text back to him and did the envelope. He took the letter and envelope and pushed sixpence across to me - the first money I earned by my writing in both senses of the word. I did the same job for him half a dozen times and then my sailor stopped coming to the Reading Room which was just as well because he never showed me replies from Agnes, if there were any, and I was running out of ideas. At the time I was grimly amused by the fact that I was earning money from my penmanship while my teachers waged an unceasing and ineffectual war against it. I wonder how Agnes managed.

There were ten days to go until the exams. We were at our sports field for athletics trials. Winners would represent the school and I hoped to be one of them. I'd run the half mile and was now doing the long jump. I was not what you'd call a brilliant long jumper but probably the best the school could come up with for the under-sixteens. It was a lean year. Facilities in those days were primitive: the long jump pit was far too narrow and the run up was on worn wet grass. My third jump. I made an over-anxious flailing effort to do a hitch-kick which I'd read about in a book. I landed awkwardly and hit my elbow, my left elbow, on the brass rule at the side of the pit. During the rest of the afternoon it became very painful and swollen. The teacher in charge advised me to go to the hospital when I got back - to be on the safe side, as he said. I could get straight off the tram from the sports field and into the London Hospital on the Whitechapel Road. At the hospital a sporty young doctor listened to my story and asked me how far I'd jumped on that third jump and I had to admit that it was such a bad jump I hadn't stopped to find out.

- I long jump for the Hospital. Hard on the ankle and the Achilles. But the elbow, that's a new one. Let's get it X-rayed.

I wanted to ask him how you jumped for a hospital but didn't want to sound stupid. The upshot was that I had broken my elbow and went home with my arm in a sling and feeling shaky. My mother took one look at the sling and, for once forgetting to drown me in sympathy, clapped her hand to her face and said,

- Your exams! How are you going to do them? Gottinue! Were you out of your mind? Fooling around just before your exams! What were you thinking of? What did they say to you at the hospital? Broken! Weh ist meine yahren, broken! Such a fine time to do long jumping. You couldn't wait till after exams, so urgent it was. You're not studying long jumping. You don't do matric in long jumping.

She sat down and rocked to and fro as though there'd been a death in the family.

- Mum, it's my left arm. The doctor showed me the X-ray. It's just a little crack. Anyone would think it had been amputated.

- God forbid. Don't even say such things. Such jokes he makes.

The next morning my form master at registration was full of concern and wanted to know the whole story. As the exams grew near most of our teachers underwent a change of heart. Slowly they changed sides and joined us as confederates in efforts to outwit the implacable examiners. By subtle analysis of past papers they tried to forecast questions and suggested ingratiating little turns of phrase we might use. My form master was not quite as frantic as my mother but shared her anxiety.

- Your writing, Rosen. It's not a work of art at the best of times but with that arm ....

- It's my left arm, sir.

- Yes, but you have to rest on it and that sling will throw you out of balance.

He spoke as though he was trying to convince himself and me, rehearsing something.

- Leave this to me. I'll write to the University.

Write to the University! To me that was like writing to God. What would he say? A few days later he beckoned to me. I went to the front of the room and he took out of an envelope a little wodge of papers.

- Read it, he said. It'll cheer you up.

I took the top sheet. It looked like a diploma with the University of London's crest at the top. It read:

This candidate 05774 has recently broken his arm. This has adversely affected his handwriting and examiners are required to take this into account when marking his papers.

My heart sang. I'd tried out my writing by then and it was the same old ugly scrawl. My arm in a sling had not made a scrap of difference. But They wouldn't know.

- There'll be one of those pinned to every paper, said my form-master. Should help a bit.

Believe it or not, he winked, that old comrades-in-crime gesture from one of my teachers! Abe wanted to know all about it.

- 'Recently broken his arm', I quoted. And it didn't say which one.

- That's one thing you can stop moaning about then, said Abe. Arm in a sling, everyone should have one. Mind you, that's what I call perfect timing.

I was so ecstatic that I felt as though I had already passed my exams. Even the examiners' iron hearts would melt when they read those notices. I could hear them saying,

- Tough on the lad. And he's churned out a readable script.

I imagined them giving me the benefit of several doubts, nudging me across a border or two and enjoying the feel of magnanimity in doing so. In each exam a slip from the University was placed on my desk and when things weren't going too well the sight of it consoled me. How could they fail a boy with a broken arm?

I passed. I got my Matric and went on to the Sixth Form. Well, you never know. Those beautiful slips may have just seen me through. Without them I might, like many of my friends, have ended up as a clerk in the City - if my writing had been good enough.

Millions of hand-written words later my writing doesn't seem to baffle anybody. In the Sixth Form I taught myself to write very small and not to swoop erratically across the page but lightly to push the pen up and down. It gradually became a sensual pleasure. It feels nice and I enjoy seeing a page of text unwinding from my pen. The word processor, calling for eight fidgety fingers, cheats me of the pleasures it took so long to develop. My thoughts don't go tap-tap. They inscribe themselves in an idiosyncratic flow. So against all the odds I end up with Roland Barthes and celebrate the 'joyous physical experience' of the calligrapher.

Zeider

We would stand by the edge of the grubby old public swimming pool drying ourselves, my zeider and I. As likely as not he would tell me once again about how he would go swimming back in der heim somewhere in Poland. I would listen to this fragment of his boyhood. Always I saw him in some Arcadian setting of endless pine trees and velvet grass sloping down to a still lake. It was always early morning. He would emerge from a log cabin, run to the water and fracture its stillness with strong strokes. He would go on swimming till he was lost to view. There were no other people, no other houses, no other movements. It was an idyll I clung to from which I had banished pogroms and poverty and the fearful little community huddled over their prayers and sewing machines.

That was my story not his. And when we went on day trips to Southend, East London's seaside, in his sixties he would set out to swim the length of the pier and back, a mile or so each way. My booba without fail went through the identical troments of anxiety. 'The meshiggenah! He's gone out too far again.' I was free from all such fears. For he was always the intrepid boy swimmer in the pure lake who always came back. And he did. And even in death still does.

Afterword: Missing Person

> Hamlet: My father, methinks I see my father.
> Horatio: O where, my lord?
> Hamlet: In my mind's eye, Horatio.

Where's your father? they used to ask me. I choked on the answer because it wasn't the name of a place and because it was a story which in my early childhood I couldn't bear to tell, a story I yearned to untell or transmute into ordinariness. Where's your father? concerned old boobas asked me in neighbours' houses and I was ashamed to have to say he wasn't where all other fathers were, where all my friends' fathers were, at their mothers' sides. Ay, ay, the boobas would say, and look down to their laps. Where's your father? asked Mr Kelk in the Elementary School when I'd written a composition about my family. I picked up my pen and wrote another sentence for him, 'My father is in America' and I spelled America wrongly and hung my head.

As far as I can tell all people without a father in the home, either because he's dead or in one way or another totally absent, know just how his ghost and the myths which cling to it stalk through their dreams, waking and sleeping, how their childhood lives are inhabited by this palpable absence. Where's your father? asks Jane Miller. She's a good friend and she says the refusal of my father to appear in the stories requires some sort of explanation. I admit you could be baffled. But that's no bad thing. Readers should be baffled. But you could also be intolerably frustrated, another matter entirely. Well, I'll set the records straight and, while I am about it, settle one or two other

Afterword: Missing Person

matters. Whether it makes any difference to how you read the stories, I can't tell.

When I was three years of age, my mother, after ten or more years in America, decided to come home to her family in the East End of London. We crossed New York where I thought the sky scrapers were going to fall on our taxi and was consoled by chunks of cake from a black leather bag. We boarded the USS *President Harding*. With us were also my older sister aged five and my younger brother, a toddler of two years. There's a photo of the four of us at the foot of a companionway. My mother looks strained and the three of us clinging to her skirts are frowning at the camera. A classic immigration picture in its way.

We had left behind my father, Morris, and two brothers, Laurie aged fifteen and Sidney, aged seventeen. The time came when my mother set about explaining why our father and brothers hadn't followed us. According to her, my father had been due to come as soon as he had scraped together the fares for the three of them. He never did and none of us in England ever saw him again. For a short while my father wrote regularly and sent some money. Then, some months after our arrival, my younger brother, Wally, died of pneumonia. It was the next part of my mother's story which stood out from the rest and which I replayed over and over again in my head. It was also the bit which I could never bear to tell when they asked, Where's your father? After my brother's death my father's letters changed from affectionate to violently recriminatory and he accused my mother of unforgivable neglect. Very soon, to her utter desolation, his letters and the money stopped, though for a while he wrote to my sister who had been a favourite and sent her a dollar or two. I was very jealous of those dollars. There was one bitter irony about my father's accusations. My mother had watched my brother die in hospital on November the eleventh, Armistice Day. She was making her way home blindly through the streets when she became aware of angry and threatening looks from the people around her. She had not heard the guns sounding for the Two Minutes Silence which meant so much in the years so close to the end of the First World War. Then it dawned on her what was happening. Only then did she begin to weep.

As we grew older we asked her why he had been so uncaring and cruel, why he had deserted us. She put it down to a wild and desperate grief at my brother's death. At other times she would claim it was beyond her understanding. We accepted her story for years and years yet anyone reading it now can see that it won't bear close scrutiny. I went on believing it well into adulthood when I eventually told myself that it didn't hang together very well. Why had she come to England without him in the first place? Was there another woman whom my mother had known about? Had there been a big final crisis quarrel? Had they been more incompatible than she had ever hinted? Her story surely must have been partly concocted to make it palatable to young children, to enable her to salvage some self-respect and she had repeated it often enough for it to become canonical. There was a hinterland I would never come to know. I never had the heart to tax her with my doubts.

Now you know why my father does not appear in my stories. In the early years of my childhood I constructed him as a handsome, powerful and loving man, a phantom who one day was certainly going to step from the shadows, reclaim us all and whisk us away to happiness. But conflicting ideas live together happily in the mind so long as an impermeable membrane keeps them apart. So I had no difficulty in believing at the same time that my mother had been tragically ill-used by him and agreed with the grown-ups at home, who saw him as a despicable wife-deserter. Then, too, there was the fact that both my brothers ran away from him, one to enlist in the American army and the other in the British army. No-one ever said why. It was always easier to keep the unblemished myth going because my mother never denounced my father. On the contrary, she fed my dreams with tales: how everyone admired his cleverness and quickness of tongue, how meticulous he was in his dress, what a fearless socialist activist and trade unionist he was, standing in local elections and victimized out of his job for organizing the union.

So there was my mother at something less than forty, only a year away from being installed in a home with a husband and five children, now a penniless single parent with her youngest dead and her two oldest turned into runaways. She had gone back to the small family house in the East End where she had grown up, ruled over by my stern matriarchal grandmother. Seven adults and a child were already somehow or another packed in.

My father remained over the years in deep freeze as a

portrait photo which I still have, showing him, a good-looking young man in his twenties with a lot of black curly hair and a high white collar, a portrait annotated by what my mother had chosen to tell. Whereas when I was young he invaded my thoughts many, many times, especially when I felt hard done by (he would have shown them), gradually he faded away into a remote figure I could contemplate without anger, hurt or embarrassment. And there had certainly been times when it was not so, when they kept asking, Where's your father?

When I was twelve, for instance, my mother was finding it desperately difficult to cope with keeping me at the grammar school, for my scholarship grant didn't cover all the costs. Winter was coming and she knew she couldn't afford the expense of winter clothes for me. She swallowed her pride and her principles at one go and applied for help from those East End benefactors, the Jewish Board of Guardians, which was run by Jews who had made it, solid loyal citizens, many of whom came from old rich Sephardic families, well-rooted in the establishment. They even looked like goyim to me. They modelled themselves on respectable English institutions and what better precedents were there than noblesse oblige and the Poor Law. They met in a very official building at the end of Petticoat Lane, full of sombre wood, polished brass and smileless portraits of Jewish eminences with trim beards and expensive tiepins. We sat in a waiting room on big chairs and my mother coached me in whispers, took off my cap and tidied my hair with her hand. Eventually I was called in. Behind a long table covered in green baize, the Guardians were waiting for me, worthies with judicious faces and gold watchchains across their waistcoats. By what processes were they appointed to dole out obligatory food to the poor and to decide who did and who did not merit a handout?

About two yards in front of the table they had placed a chair. Sit down, Harold, someone was saying. I felt humiliated already, vulnerable, afraid of saying the wrong thing. Then came the grilling. Who lived at our house? How many were in work? What was the name of my school? What subjects was I studying? Did I get good marks? How much did my scholarship grant amount to? And so on. Then someone asked,

- Your father, my boy, what is his trade?

I sweated and swallowed. I groped.

- He's ....my father is .... my father's job. He isn't here. I don't know his job.

- Well, where exactly is your father?

The old unanswerable question. Before I could answer there was whispering back there and shuffling of dossiers.

- Never mind that now. Do you have to pay for your school textbooks?

The Guardians deliberated and they gave my mother some vouchers for a suit and footwear. Money might so easily be misspent. The vouchers were only valid at one establishment in the Lane which turned out to be a kind of charity depot the Guardians had set up. Everything was on shelves in boxes and parcels. A sad little man took my measurements.

- The suit mebbe you won't like. We're not Cecil Gee's. But like iron it is. You can't wear it out if you try. And the boots, you wouldn't go to the Palais in them but for lobbuses in the school yard ....

He patted my back, consoling me. He was right. The suit was made of thick brown indestructible cloth and I only saw its like when I went with a team to play chess in the Jewish Boys Orphanage in Norwood. All the boys wore suits just like that there. The heavy black boots I had to wear all that winter even though for us the boot age had long since passed.

I eventually composed a formula to deal with Where's your father? Without batting an eyelid I would say, I haven't got a father. This left them to decide whether I was an orphan or a bastard. I think they usually settled for orphan, more comfortable all round. Sometimes I brazenly said, he's dead, which cut out any further questions.

- Dead? Uvver sholem, they'd say, and leave it at that.

I see it all differently now, untinged, I hope, with self-pity. We were not an uniquely ill-fated family nor particularly unlucky. All over the world millions and millions of families and bits of families were and still are trekking across continents and oceans, harried by others and driven on by their fears and ambitions. How many wives lose their husbands, how many children their parents and each other? How many survivors would be glad to settle for one parent alive or a sister or brother? Besides, although something inescapably tragic clings about my memories of my mother's life - it is, after all, a sad story - she recovered rapidly from her disaster, as my stories show. It's true that she is sometimes a partly fictional figure in them but there's enough to show what a fighter she was. It was, after all, through her that I became a communist. She was the one above all who propelled me against the odds to go on to university education. Quite simply she believed in learning. When I was in the Sixth Form I read Frazer's *Golden Bough* and thought myself rarely intellectual. I took it home and she said, Fine book, and began talking about it. Of course I was irritated. And here I am, what they call an Emeritus Professor and I still believe we need a better and quite different kind of society and I don't care whether you call it socialist or communist. I chafe inside the Labour Party, lamenting its timidities and mourning the days when there was a viable alternative. My mother said to me when she was old,

- I used to be sure that I'd see socialism here, in my day. Anyone can see that I won't. But you, you will live to see it in your day.

At my age that doesn't look likely and things don't look too promising for my sons. Perhaps I'll say the same as she did to my grandchildren sometime, but, if I do, it will be much more tentatively.

Everything I've worked for in education I can trace back to its beginnings in my family and its fierce radicalism and dogged hope which themselves grew out of an East End humming with politics. I don't want to explain everything in the stories which might give rise to questions. They must, like any stories, speak for themselves. In any case, I've not written an autobiography. I don't think I could - far too daunting. I have only rooted about in the depths of my past and grubbed up fragments which speak to me. It turned out they were all about my childhood and more particularly about my schooling. That must be because, rather late in the day, I revisited that distant world and interrogated it. That was when some of us were asking questions about the education of children from immigrant families who were settling into communities. What about their languages? What did it mean to be a member of a minority, to meet undisguised and dangerous hostility? I realised I'd been there already in my childhood. I used my scrutiny to help me understand bilingualism and what it means to be what Jane Miller calls a hybrid. When in the sixties and seventies it became fashionable to talk about the linguistic deprivation of the working class, I remembered the eloquence of the people amongst whom I grew up, not only those in the rag trade but also people like the dockers who sat in our living room and joked, told tales and wrote leaflets.

If I write about narrative these days, as well as engage in it, it's because, on my return journey to the East End, I recalled that the air was always thick with stories and the mealtimes were loud with them.

You can pin on me the neat label of scholarship boy if you like, but before you tidy me away into that stereotype and ask me to be grateful, remember that I had more than one schooling, my elementary school, my grammar school, the university, the Communist Party and, as I slowly came to realise, that vibrant academy, the Jewish East End. Jane is right. I am a hybrid.

Avrum's Overcoat

Once upon a time - no, not as long ago as that - I should say years and years ago. Well, more exactly some time in the thirties (don't make me out a liar for a few years more or less), they were sitting around the dominoes table in the social room of the Garment Workers' Union, sipping lemon tea and nibbling kichelech and they got round to arguing about who was the best tailor they'd ever come across, like others argue about the best centre forward or the best violinist. My Uncle Max was there and of course he said, 'I know who was the best tailor ever!' and he told them what he's told us so many times that we could tell it along with him.

Was Avrum Plotnik a great tailor! He could fit a jacket for you like you'd been poured into it, make a nobody look like a somebody. His wife, Yetta, swore that in a room full of people she could pick out a Plotnik jacket. Maybe, maybe. But if he was a tailor in a million it didn't stop him from being poor. There weren't many people around any more who'd pay good money for a suit of fourteen ounce wool, with hand-stitched edges, hand-sewn button-holes and three fittings into the bargain. There wasn't that kind of money about. So even the flash boys along the Whitechapel Road and the frumme whitebeards in the schul would wear their suits for much longer or, more likely, buy readymades from the Fifty Shilling tailors by Aldgate Station like the goyim who didn't know any better.

So Avrum was beginning to despair of ever making a decent living. And he had even started talking to Yetta in the evenings about turning his hand to something else - a fabrics stall in the market, selling drapery from door to door on the never-never, even taking a job as a schlepper in Cousin Solly's shop in the Lane. A tear or two was shed but in the finish he couldn't bring himself to part with his beloved sewing machine, tailor's dummy, the big pressing irons, the brass-handled shears and his boxes of flat, sharp-edged chalks.

It happened that at this very time Yankel Goldfarb made a killing. I should tell you that Yankel Goldfarb was a bit of a mystery. When anyone asked what he did for a living he'd give a bit of a smile and say, 'I buy a bit and I sell a bit, I buy and I sell.' Suspicious people said, 'God knows where he gets that dreck he hawks around. Not from the Houndsditch Warehouse, that's for sure.' Suddenly Yankel was in the money. No one knew how. There was talk of bankrupt stock but no one knew for sure. He moved from his house in Varden Street to Golders Green. Like everyone said, he'd become a ganzer macher, a big shot. All of a sudden there's his picture in the *Jewish Chronicle* and *Die Zeit* as the well-known businessman, Y. Goldfarb, making a donation to the Jewish old people's home in Brighton or opening a new synagogue in Finchley. Eventually he was in the daily papers, laughing with politicians, footballers and men in DJs with smiles like chainsaws. If you looked very closely at the pictures and you knew anything about such things, you might say, 'He may be a bit of a gunuf but he knows how to choose a tailor' and if Yetta happened to be there she'd say, 'Of course he does. That's a Plotnik suit. Anyone can see that.' Yes, it was true. Plotnik had become Goldfarb's tailor.

When Goldfarb made his killing that nobody asks too many questions about these days, and began mixing with the high and mighty, he realised that he had to change a thing or two, to talk differently, to walk differently and to dress differently. The talking and walking he paid good money to make English. But when it came to clothes he knew just what to do about them. He wasn't going to be conned into rushing off to Savile Row. A good East End tailor it had to be.

He employed at that time a kind of secretary, agent, public relations man, sniffer out of trouble, legal eagle. He'd taken him straight from college, licked him into shape and showed him a thing or two they don't teach you at Oxford. He learnt fast so that press men and a politician or two got a bit jumpy when they spoke to him. We don't have to get nervous about him because he's going to leave this story very soon and Goldfarb won't be around much longer either.

Goldfarb had noticed that his right-hand man wore suits that were the envy of even the most well-heeled of his - what did he call them? - business associates. One day he said to him,

- Stephen, my boy, that suit you're wearing. Tell me who made it.

- You wouldn't know him, Mr Goldfarb.

- Did I ask you if I knew him? Who is this needle-pusher and why are you making such a secret about it?

- Mr Goldfarb, you know very well my people come from Old Montague Street. So why shouldn't I know a good tailor? He's a relative of sorts, lives in Mount Street behind the London Hospital. When I had my first long-trouser suit (my barmitzvah, of course) my mother said, 'It's Avrum Plotnik or nobody'. I should tell you, though, he's just a poor little tailor who works out of his front room.

- Stephen, the time it takes you to spit out an answer to a simple question I could do ten thousand quids worth of business.

So that's how Avrum got called to Goldfarb's office in Holborn and stood in front of a desk you could have played table tennis on.

- A double-breasted suit, Mr Goldfarb? Six button jacket? Contrast silk lining? A smart charcoal flannel? Inch-and-a-half turn ...?

- Plotnik, Plotnik, Goldfarb put an arm round his shoulder, you want to keep this job? Do me a favour - think a bit bigger. It's a whole wardrobe I'm asking you to make and I'm not talking about cabinet-making.

A whole wardrobe turned out to be five suits, two winter overcoats, one spring overcoat, sports jackets, a blazer, trousers galore. Avrum rushed to and fro with sample swatches of cloth and put them on Goldfarb's desk - cashmeres, serges, meltons, gabardines, corduroys, worsteds, baratheas, cavalry twills, Norfolk tweeds, Harris tweeds, Donegal tweeds, in pin-stripes, dog-tooth, Lovat, herringbone, pepper-and-salt and checks. Goldfarb banged his desk, jutted his jaw and browbeat Avrum as he browbeat everyone else.

- Don't forget, he said, I can buy tailors like you two-a-penny. The East End's lousy with them. They'd give an arm and a leg to make me a waistcoat. They'd sell their mothers for the whole wardrobe. So don't bring me schmutters I wouldn't be seen dead in. And no more hairy tweeds that make me look like a gorilla.

Avrum held his tongue. He knew by now that when Goldfarb had finished throwing his weight about he'd make a choice. And that's how he got the commission for the wardrobe and I don't mean cabinet-making. For the first time in his life he was making good money. In fact, once Goldfarb started wearing his suits he couldn't resist boasting about his tailor and Avrum got more orders than he could cope with. One day he came home from a fitting and Yetta cleared a space in the front room he worked in. She needed to. There were bolts of cloth higgledy-piggledy on the sideboard, the table was covered in brown paper patterns and there was wadding and canvas all over the chairs. On the mantelpiece were rows and rows of cotton reels and white boxes of buttons, black, brown leather and brass sewn onto cards. The floor was covered in snippings and clippings and the tailor's dummy looked at them from a corner wearing a half-finished jacket covered in white basting stitches. Yetta brushed a space clear and put out some food.

- Good tailoring never came from an empty belly, she said, so enough work for one day. Have some borsht. Half way through eating Avrum stopped.

- You know something, Yetta? I've made enough with my needle and shears (and I haven't forgotten your felling and basting and button-holing) to do something I've wanted to do ever since I became a master tailor.

- You mean go mad and go to Brighton for the day and eat like a horse at Mrs Levi's restaurant?

- No need to mock, Yetta. We can go any time we like and for a fortnight maybe. But you know what they say, 'Who shaves the barber?' For thirty years I've made overcoats enough for a regiment of soldiers. To make myself a quality overcoat there's never been a time. That one I wear came down to me from my great uncle Izzy, uvver sholem. Quality, yes, but I never liked the style. That belt with the big buckle and the buttons like cartwheels. And patch pockets! Makes me look like a bookie or a boxing promoter. So I tell you what. I'm going to make an overcoat for myself like you never saw.

- Why not? said Yetta. If that gangster Goldfarb can have umpteen overcoats hanging up to try and make him look like Lord Muck, can't an honest tailor have one overcoat to make him feel like a real mensch on a winter's day?

- Goldfarb's no gangster. Shady dealings, maybe. Driving

hard bargains when he's put the frighteners on, faulty goods sold as perfect, funny money, but he ....

- Anyone who makes that kind of money by me is a gangster.

- Forget that momser. I'm thinking about that overcoat already.

He sipped his lemon tea, closed his eyes and sighed with pleasure.

So Avrum Plotnik made himself an overcoat, an overcoat like a work of art. You could have hung it in a gallery. There's not a lot I can tell you about it because a beautiful overcoat you wouldn't hang in a gallery, would you? No, you have to see it in action with a person inside, moving along the street. In any case, what no one would actually see was the love and joy which went into every stitch. I remember Avrum's bitter curses in the summers when he made overcoats for the winter trade. At the end of the day his arms ached and his hands trembled. But the making of his own beloved overcoat drew not a complaint from him. This much I can tell you about it. It was made of the finest dark brown melton with a Prussian collar, raglan sleeves, turn-up cuffs and double stitched seams. The lining was a dark red shot silk and the buttons leather knots and I can tell you when he first wore it, heads turned. He wore it everywhere, to schul, of course, to barmitzvahs, to weddings, to funerals. In fact he wore it whenever he left the house. He wore it even when he went up the street to buy an evening paper. He loved that overcoat so much he could scarcely bear to take it off when he came indoors. He sweltered in it till late spring and when summer came he couldn't wait for the cool days of autumn.

Small wonder, then, that the day came when the overcoat began to show signs of wear. The nap began to go, the cuffs frayed and the collar was stained with sweat. The hem was discoloured and loose threads hung from it. Avrum could not admit this to himself. He walked about in his coat as though it still shone in its first glory. But when he caught sight of himself in shop windows he quickly turned his eyes away and poor Yetta, she was torn. She didn't need telling how Avrum adored that overcoat but she was ashamed that he walked about looking shabby and neglected. Mrs Michaelson - who else? - said to her one day,

- What's the matter with Plotnik? He walks around looking like an alter schnorrer begging for pennies. A real nebbich, and him a tailor good enough for that Yankel Goldfarb.

That was the last straw. That day she held up Avrum's coat in front of him.

- It's no good. This coat is so threadbare it's not fit to be made into shmutters for cleaning the floor. You waiting for it to fall off your back or for the lobbuses to shout after you in the street? Come on, admit it.

- I admit it. I admit it.

He took it from her and was ready to throw it away. He picked it up and looked it over carefully from top to bottom, from back to front.

- It's true. It's finished, he said. Well, not quite. From this I could make a decent jacket.

He cut out the areas which were not worn or stained and from them there emerged a single-breasted jacket. A bit thick for a jacket, maybe, but for Avrum it was a kind of resurrection of his wonderful overcoat. He wore the jacket just as he had the overcoat, everyday, everywhere and for everything. He kept it going for as long as he could. When it was out at elbow he made neat oval leather patches and he sewed narrow leather strips round the frayed cuffs. But its time also came. It was a sad sight, dilapidated, grimy and shapeless. Yetta said quietly to him,

- Avrum, the jacket is done for. Don't go round looking like a down-and-out.

- You're right, Yetta. It's only fit for Stern the rag-picker.

He took it from its hook and he was just going to stuff it into a carrier bag when he took another look at it. I dunno, he thought, done for? Well, not quite. From this I could make a decent waistcoat. He took some rough measurements with the span of his hand. He then rescued enough cloth for the two front panels of the waistcoat. That's all he needed, for the back was made of new black twill.

Well, the waistcoat didn't see a year out. The bits he'd salvaged were not as good as they looked. If you'd have held them up to the light you could have read a newspaper through them and between you and me, Avrum had a bit of a paunch so lockshen soup got dribbled down the front and other schmalzy spillings left their trademarks. Not that Yetta and he didn't try to get these embarrassments cleaned off, but that only meant that the cloth got more and more worn and finally so shabby that Yetta had to say,

- Avrum, that waistcoat has died. Bury it.

Avrum was silent at first and then took a last look at it. Takke, he said, it's all over with it. Then he took another look....

Well, not quite. From this I could make a decent little skull cap, a yamalka with a strong lining.

And that's what he did.

Mind you, the cap didn't last very long - how could it? It had served its time and reached the end of its days. Yetta said,

- Avrum, with a needle you can work miracles but all the same I can't let you sit and daven in that. For praying and reading the holy books you must be covered right. How you can bear to put the praying shawl over it I don't know.

- You're right, said Avrum, the cap must go. Its duties are finished .... Well, not quite. From this I could make a decent little cloth-covered button.

So he clipped out just enough to make a button. He pinned the button to the lapel of his jacket where he could always see it out of the corner of his eye. He loved that little button. Sometimes he'd rub it with his thumb as though it brought him good luck or warded off the evil eye.

But he couldn't go on rubbing it forever. It began to fray away. The threads parted and stuck out round the edges and the blackish metal underneath showed through till it wasn't a cloth button any more. Avrum didn't wait for Yetta to protest. He unpinned the button and held it in the middle of his palm for a long time. Then he said to it,

- Little button, little survivor, in spite of everything you must go, for this is the end of the road. Well, not quite. From this button could I make a story! And that's the story I've just told you.

The Story of the Story

There is always the story of the story, even several stories.

We had been at a storyteller's gathering, Betty Rosen and I, and had been in different groups. In the car going home she had given me a minimalist version of a story she had heard told by Patrick Ryan, a well-known storyteller. It had no specific geographical or ethnic setting but I felt instantly on hearing the very condensed version of the story of the tailor and his overcoat that it was asking to be made into a much longer version about a Jewish tailor in the East End where I grew up. I had about ten lines scribbled in the car in a very small notebook. This became a story told by my fictitious Uncle Max about the master tailor, Avrum Plotnik.

I was honour bound to send my version to Patrick Ryan. He responded warmly and, as I have since discovered, typically. He told me his story of the story of the story:

> I heard David Holt tell it at a workshop for teachers at the Old Town School of Folk Music in Chicago. David Told me that he'd learned the story and the methodology of his workshops from a woman named Nancy Schimmel. In the late seventies Nancy wrote a book on storytelling which became a sort of bible, Just Enough to Make a Story ....

I should have chased up the book but procrastination took over. Almost a year later an American woman came to see us. She was engaged in a personal and serious investigation of storytelling for a piece she was writing. We spent a sunny afternoon in the garden sharing hunches, ideas, pleasures. It turned out that she was also about to embark on a doctorate and when she returned home she wrote and asked me if I would be one of her supervisors. The letter contained relevant documents. She threw in for good measure a little gift, Nancy Schimmel's Introduction to the book Patrick Ryan had mentioned. That rang a bell, of course. Her economic version of the story begins:

> In a village there once lived a poor tailor. He had made overcoats for many people, but he had never made one for himself, though an overcoat was just what he wanted.

and ends:

> ....he could see there was just enough left of that button to make a story so he made a story out of it and I just told it to you.

She goes on to tell us that she first met the story when 'I heard someone sing a Yiddish folk song at a concert and explain in English what the song says.' At this point I remembered a book my son had given me, an anthology of

Yiddish folk songs, *Voices of a People*. I searched through it and found that it contained the song but, strangely, only the first and last verses. Here's the translation of the last one:

> I have nothing left of the ancient stuff
> It hasn't a whole stitch in it
> Therefore I made up my mind
> To make a little song out of nothing

Now you know why Avrum's Overcoat is not my story and why it is my story. No matter what the story, that's always the way of it.

The Tailor Who Couldn't Tell Stories

The last story in Henry Glassie's collection *Irish Folk Tales* (Penguin 1987) is called 'The Man who had no Story'. I liked it so much that at the first opportunity I told it at a teachers' workshop in Leicester. I wasn't very satisfied. It's a story about Brian O'Braonachain and is as Irish as that name. There's a wake, a mass and osier cutting. Then I heard Betty Rosen tell a version of 'The Giant over the Mountain' in which a very short tale which happened nowhere became a long story about Gwyneth in a Welsh fishing village like the ones near to where she grew up. So I switched the Irish story to the places and people where I grew up, and felt much happier telling it. That's how Brian, the osier cutter, became Chaim, the tailor, and the wake became a 'briss', a circumcision. Which is what has always happened to stories.

There was once a little Jewish tailor called Chaim who lived in a house just behind the Philpot Street Synagogue. Suits and overcoats he could make like nobody else. But he fell on hard times. He wasn't the only one. The tailoring everyone said had one foot in the grave. Suits fit for a Rothschild gathered dust. Seeing his family suffering, he made up his mind to try something different to make ends meet. In the small yard at the back of his house nothing grew in the dusty black soil except some struggling weeds and a large patch of a tough plant with long coarse leaves. You wouldn't give it a second look but Chaim knew that it was from the roots of this plant that you

The Tailor Who Coudn't Tell Stories

could make chrane, horseradish sauce with beetroot. It had foot-long knobbly roots which you grated while the tears ran from your eyes. Every Friday before shabbas came in he had seen his wife Ruchele grate the chrane, tears running down her cheeks. With a little beetroot it would be ready for the shabbas chicken. So Chaim, knowing that shabbas without chrane is like pesach without matzos, set himself up a little business. The bespoke tailor became a bespoke chrane maker and he sold his little jars from an old pram on a corner in Wentworth Street. Do I need to tell you he didn't make a fortune, move to Golders Green, and make good marriages for his daughters? But he scraped a living.

Poor Chaim, he was soon in deep trouble again. He had used up every root in the yard. He watched his stock of jars dwindling to a dozen or so. There was nothing for it but to look for another source of supply. But what little East End tailor knew where to find chrane growing? Poor Chaim couldn't have told you where to find an oak tree or a dandelion. What should he do? Take a bus to Epping Forest and search for the long coarse leaves? He certainly hadn't seen any in Victoria Park. He was in despair until he remembered Mendele. If you believed the yuchners in Hessel Street market you would believe that Mendele had once been a respected rabbi, but because he had dabbled in the cabbala and god knows what black arts, they threw him out. Still, Chaim thought to himself, a clever man is a clever man, a malamed is a malamed, even if he can't turn beigels into golden bracelets.

So Chaim took himself to Mendele's dark little room crammed with old books, sheets and sheets of notes scribbled in Hebrew with strange signs which Chaim had never seen before. When Mendele had let him in, he poured out his story. Mendele listened without saying a word. He just sat there wrinkling up his leathery face, scratched behind his yamulka and twiddled his beard.

- Chaim, he said, I can tell you where to find this plant in abundance, as easily as I can tell you how to get from here to the shvitzig in Brick Lane.

- Tell, tell, said Chaim.

- There's more to it than that. Such good fortune doesn't drop in a man's way like manna. The manna days are over and done with. The Red Sea don't part for us any more.

Quaking, Chaim reached for his purse, knowing it was unlikely he could offer enough.

- Put it away, put it away, Mendele said irritably. I will direct you to a place where you will find enough chrane to last you till the Messiah comes. You know the old Jewish burial ground? Alongside is a plot of waste ground. Go and look there. Only that waste ground must be treated with as much respect as the burial ground itself. Just remember one thing though, and he looked Chaim straight in the eye, What will happen when you start rooting around I cannot say.

- What can happen ? Chaim's voice was a whisper. Mendele was already turning to his books. He behaved as if Chaim wasn't there. Not a word could be dragged from him. Chaim ran from the room, praying all the way home. He told Ruchele what Mendele had said.

- That meshigenah, she said, You trust him? I've heard about him. His head is like an old booba's bag stuffed full of bits and pieces. All the same don't go up to the cemetery. The evil eye looks upon it. Old Chainik, may his soul rest in peace, once walked past there ...

- Enough! Enough! said Chaim. Make a couple of platzels with chopped herring or something, I'm going right now. I'll dig out as much as I can carry.

Ruchele, seeing there was no help for it, put up some lunch for him and he took a large sack and the fork he had used to dig his own chrane. A little anxious in heart, he set out for the old burial ground. As soon as he arrived, he rushed over to the waste ground. Sure enough there was clump after clump of sturdy horseradish plants. He threw down his lunch bag and straight away got on with the the business of digging out the roots, thinking all the time of jars and jars of chrane ready for sale. After a while he began to slow down. He stopped work, gathered his precious roots and crammed them into the sack. It was almost more than he could carry. Ai, Mendele, he thought, they can say what they like but those books and that little head have worked a little miracle for me. He suddenly felt hungry and sat down, opened his lunch bag and munched away on his chopped herring platzels. While he was eating he felt the sweat he had worked up go cold on him and he noticed a sharp wind was blowing through the old gravestones and bending the leaves of the horseradish. It was getting misty too. Then it grew darker, then darker until he found himself platzel in hand in pitch darkness. The wind grew ferocious and so powerful was it that he was suddenly whisked up into the air and twirled round

The Tailor Who Coudn't Tell Stories

and round, his arms and legs flailing about. He turned head over heels again and again. That Mendele and his cursed books, he kept thinking. May the cholera take him.

Soon he felt himself coming to earth and he landed gently as a feather from a passing bird. Relieved as he was to have come safely to earth, he was still dismayed to find himself in pitch darkness. But the cobbles of a road were under his feet and after a while he could see in the distance a bright light. Where there's light there's people, he thought. I'll get out of this schemozzle yet. So he stepped briskly along the street, dimly aware of houses and shops on either side of him. Not a sound came from one of them, not a window or door was open. He pressed on until he came to the house where light was streaming through the open door. He could see, sitting one each side of a bright fire, an old man and an old woman.

- Come in, come in, the woman said. Take a chair to the fire and sit down. I'll get you a bite to eat. She set before him a plate of wurst, pickled cucumber, cold salt beef and black rye bread.

- May your children have good luck and grandchildren also, said Chaim, his mind still trying to catch up with events. They smiled and watched him eat.

When he had finished, the old man said,
- It's too early for bed, so tell us a story.
- Me! said Chaim. I could make you a suit like you wouldn't find in Savile Row but tell a story, never. I've listened to Schmiel the Shikke tell hundreds when he's had one or two but I can't remember a single one. Bella with the egg stall can tell stories would make the eyes pop out of your head. But me.... no, I like to listen.

- Oh well, said the woman in a bit of a huff, supper you can eat, your toes you can toast in front of the fire but a story you can't manage. Maybe Mr Gentleman you could manage to fetch in a bucket of coal from the shed in the backyard.

Chaim was only too willing. He picked up the coal bucket, went out to the shed, filled the bucket with coal, stood it down and paused for breath. As he did so, once again he was swept off his feet, whisked into the air and buffetted about. He turned over and over, half falling, half floating. He landed lightly in pitch darkness. In the darkness he saw a bright light, much brighter than the first time. 'Where there's light....' he said to himself. Once again he headed down a street in which every house was dark, bolted and barred. He arrived at the open door of a big house. From inside he could hear the sound of a baby crying and a babble of excited voices. He walked into a large room and he could tell in a moment from the table full of food and the way the men had grouped themselves around the baby that any minute there was going to be a circumcision. And then he noticed, amongst the women seated in a huddle at the far end of the room, a beautiful dark-haired young woman who beckoned to him and had him stand beside her.

At that very moment a big fellow with a black beard shouted out,

- The moel is ten minutes late already. A disgrace. Maybe we could get old Gottlieb.

Just as someone made for the door the beautiful girl at Chaim's side stepped forward and said,

- No need. Chaim here is the best moel from Stamford Hill to Whitechapel.

She gave him a little push.

- Me! said Chaim. Are you meshiggah? I would do the little baby a terrible injury. God forbid. Me with a surgeon's knife! I wouldn't trust myself to bandage a cut finger. Anyway I can't stand the sight of blood.

- What sort of mishegas is this? The young woman said in his ear sharply, Don't make me a liar in front of all these people.

Suddenly Chaim found himself in the moel's garments, a scalpel in his hand. Without a moment's hesitation he stepped forward and deftly removed the baby's foreskin. As is the custom, the baby screamed its head off.

- Shush tatele, said the baby's father, well satisfied that the deed was at last done.

- Now, said the big man with the beard, if we had someone who could play the fiddle. A briss without music, who ever heard of such a thing? Such a pity.

The beautiful woman next to Chaim spoke up again.

- Don't worry, don't worry. Chaim here can play like Heifetz. He'll have you tapping your feet and dancing in no time.

- Fiddler! said Chaim, A nice bit of fiddling is a blessing but if I scraped a fiddle you'd all go running out of the room. To me a fiddler is a miracle.

- A little joke, said the woman. He loves a little joke. Turning to Chaim she whispered,

\- So you want to make me an idiot in front of all the guests.

In a flash Chaim was standing there fiddle and bow at the ready. He began playing.

\- It's true, someone said, Like Heifetz. Such a fiddler you don't hear at every briss. The big man called for silence. You know, he said, if Itzig's son, Avrum - the one with all those degrees - were here, we would have a lovely speech. Like to finish things off. Such a pity.

\- A speech, said the woman. You think we won't have a speech when we have here Chaim, the best speechmaker in the whole community.

Chaim mumbled and muttered.

\- Speeches yet. Anyone who knows me will tell you I wouldn't say boo to a goose. They say I'm like Bontshe Schweig in the story, a man of very few words. If I start talking in company, my throat goes dry. I try to say something and words don't come out.

\- Such modesty you only find in great men, said the woman to the guests. In Chaim's ear she said, How will I hold my head up again? Mrs Stein would give an arm and a leg to see me made such a fool.

Chaim climbed on a chair and was soon delivering a speech full of jokes and witticisms and some philosophising about life which everyone liked because it was a bit over their heads. When he started quoting Maimonides they glowed.

\- Ach, such a speech you only hear once in a lifetime.

It seemed to Chaim that the room had become unbearably stuffy. He went to stand in the doorway for a breath of fresh air. As he stood there that strange sensation came on again and he was once more snatched into the air and flung hither and thither. This time when he landed he found himself back at the shed with the bucket of coal in front of him. Though he was a bit confused at first, he soon gathered his wits, picked up the bucket of coal and went back into the house. The old couple were sitting by the fire exactly as he had left them. He put the bucket on the hearth and drew a chair up to the fire. After a few moments silence the old man said,

\- Soon time for bed. So tell us Chaim, can you tell us a story?

\- Oy have I got a story, have I got a story, said Chaim and he told them everything which had happened since he went out to get coal.

- A story is like good luck, said the old woman. Now wherever you go, if someone asks for a story, they'll know you're a storyteller for sure.

They had a supper that night like it was a festival — chicken soup with kneidlech, liver rissoles with latkes and sweet honig lekach to finish up with. They put Chaim in a feather bed and he slept and slept. He dreamt that a big man with a beard was buying one of his bespoke suits and stroking it like it was a precious fur. When he woke up he wasn't in the feather bed anymore but in the waste ground next to the graveyard. By his side was his lunch bag, his digging fork and the sackful of horseradish roots. He picked them up and headed for Ruchele and home.

And I can tell you. he hasn't needed to fill another jar with chrane from that day to this, by my life so sure.

Yiddish – English Glossary

alter	old
barmitzvah	religious initiation for 13-year-old boys
beigel	ring-shaped bread roll
blintzes	pancakes with a filling
booba	grandmother
Bontshe Schweig	Bontshe the Silent (or Meek) in Sholem Aleichem's story
borsht	beetroot soup
briss	circumcision ceremony
chap	grab, snatch
chazan	cantor in the synagogue
chrane	a sharp relish made of grated horseradish and beetroot
chutzpah	bare-faced impudence
chuzza	a pig (literal and metaphorical)
daven	to pray
dreck	filth, worthless rubbish
dumm	stupid
frumme	orthodox, pious
ganzer macher	self-important big-shot

gottinue!	my God!
gott sei dank	God be thanked
goy, pl.goyim	gentile(s)
gunuf, pl.gunovim	thief, thieves
gutgas	trousers
der heim	the land of origin, usu. Poland or Russia
honig lekach	honey cake
katzenkopf	cat's head i.e. a fool
kichelech	little cakes
kishkas	guts
kneidlech	a dumpling for soup
knucker	a show-off, self-regarding braggart
latkes	potato pancakes
lobbus	a bit of a hooligan, a bad lad
lockshen	noodles, usu. to put in soup
malamed	a teacher, an unworldly scholar
matzos	unleavened bread
mensh	a man, a real man
meshiggah	mad
mishegas	madness, clowning
moel	the approved performer of cirmumcision
naar	a fool
nebbich	a pitiful person; (as an exclamation) what a shame! poor thing! etc.
Pesach	Passover
platzel	a flat bread roll
Shabbas	Sabbath
shikke	a drunk
schlepp	to drag
schlepper	one outside a shop to pull in custom

schloch	a clumsy, inept person
schmalz	melted fat
schmendrik	a fool
schmeryl	a fool
schmutter	a rag; (+ trade) the garment industry
schnorrer	a scrounger
shtummer	a dumb person
schul	synagogue
schvitzig	steam baths
takke	just so, that's true
tatele	an endearment addressed to a small boy
tuchas lecher	arse-licker
uvver sholem	(of the dead) rest in peace
yamalka	skull cap
yeshiva bocher	a Talmudic scholar, a swot
yuchner	a busybody, a gossip
zeider	grandfather

Song Titles and Phrases

As der rebbe Eli Meli is gevoren sehr gefreli:
When the rabbi Eli Meli got very jolly (i.e. drunk)

Herrt a meisser kindele:	Listen to a story, children
Weh ist meine yahren:	Woe upon my years!

The Politics Of Writing

This paper is the prosing of a hefty fistful of notes for a lecture I gave in Detroit in 1983 to the National Council of Teachers of English.

Let's begin with a story with a happy ending. On a certain day in autumn for certain, for in the Bronx or Brixton we have to wait until the harvest is in, Little Audrey begins her first day at school. The chemistry of a long-drawn-out metamorphosis is launched. Up to this point Little Audrey has relied on the mere accident of birth, the chance encounters of everyday life and on the unplanned and frequently repulsive didactics of the subculture (a euphemism for deviant subgroups) for her education. But now, if all goes well, our infant is going to be socialized at state expense, that is, she is going to be inducted into the mainstream culture. And if there's one thing we can be sure of it is that a central pillar of that culture is literacy. I must rush towards our happy ending - when our infant emerges at the other end, she will not only be civilized into being a good citizen but will also have acquired the very special, indeed superordinate, achievement of literacy. As numerous experts have told us this leads to profound changes in the human psyche. Little Audrey will have acquired, so they say, abstract, context-free thought, rationality, powers of criticism, detachment, in sum a totally new way of looking at the world which will change the whole cast of her cognitive processes (see Ong 1982, Goody 1977, Olson 1977 and others). And all that at the mere cost of learning to read and write. Since we are concerned today specifically with learning to write, let me cite

Olson's well-known essay, 'From utterance to text', as typical.

> .... the invention of the alphabetic writing system gave to Western culture many of its predominant features including an altered conception of language and altered conception of rational man. These effects came about, in part, from the creation of explicit, autonomous statements, statements dependent upon an explicit writing system, the alphabet and an explicit form of argument, the essay. (p. 262)

O lucky and thrice-blessed Little Audrey!

Forgive my sceptical tone so far. But remember we are a special group, very much predisposed not to question the value of writing (we earn our living by it!) and we are anxious to learn about better ways of teaching it. I too believe in the value of writing but in nothing like the unproblematic way that Olson and others do. So let me try to disturb you a little. I will add a little to my story. Little Audrey had been introduced to the special cultural joys described by Olson and at the end of a year or so she was able to write the words in the blank spaces in standardized tests. She had thus 'an altered conception of rational man'. One day a gentle old French professor called Michel de Certeau was visiting her classroom and saw her to be engaged on a writing task. He walked up to her and whispered in her ear,

> 'To write .... is to be forced to march through enemy territory'.

Little Audrey never forgot the professor's words even when (especially when!) she was filling in her tax form, writing assignments in freshman English and applying for research grants. She had by then of course bought a copy of de Certeau's remarkable book, *The practice of everyday life* (1984). I shall come back to his disturbing and outrageous notion but for the moment I shall assume that you find the idea a little odd (at the very least) and perhaps lunatic. Certainly it does not match the enthusiasms of Olson and others who hint at no such thing. But if you find the idea odd, I ask you to recollect having to write recently a piece of formal prose - a report, an official letter of some length, the minutes of a meeting or, better still, a letter of application for a job. My guess is that you experienced a kind of tension between what you wanted to say and what you knew were the expectations of how you should say it. A self-censorship produces a calcified prose you would gladly disown.

There is after all a common way of treating socialization: writing is clearly a form of socialization though it is often not looked at in that way. It is a socialization into a specific kind of literate culture. We all know that from the moment of their birth all children have to be changed from little animals into social human beings. One way (not mine) of looking at this process is to say quite simply that the complex organism we call society, heterogeneous and elusive as it may be, is sustained, confirmed and reproduced by a set of norms-and-rules and that basically a child's socialization consists in learning those rules and governing his/her practices in the light of them. There are obviously refinements on this model, e.g. the incorporation of some diversity of norms-and-rules and sub-systems; but in general, as Agnes Heller puts it,

> professionalism [in the social sciences] .... views society as it exists, the status quo as a datum .... [it] is concerned to investigate but not to change, at most to improve the way society works.

To put it another way, the social system is looked upon as lying in wait for us with a whole apparatus of practices, values, beliefs etc and we are irresistibly drawn into them. Very briefly let me say what I think is wrong with that model.

(a) The social system confronts us at a particular moment in history.
(b) Because power is unequally distributed, some practices will be given high value not because of intrinsic merit but because they are validated by the powerful.
(c) Many of the most important practices in the culture help to keep the powerful powerful though they are never presented that way but rather as universal or value-free or in their final state of evolution.
(d) The model does not offer us any understanding of conflict of values except as deviance, maladjustment etc.

To come down to earth from those generalizations, let me cite an instance of how the discourse of social scientists is paralleled in everyday discourse in one of its most common locations - school. I borrow the example from Henry Giroux (1983).

Mrs Caplow is a kindergarten teacher working on a unit devoted to citizenship.The aim of the unit, she says, is to teach 'respect for the law'. As part of her scheme she appoints a 'sheriff' from among the children. The sheriff interprets this by pushing and shoving the children who step out of line. Here is an exchange conducted for the researcher's benefit.

> Mrs Caplow: David, can you tell Mr Rist why you are wearing the star?
> David: Cause I the sheriff.
> Mrs C: Can you tell him how you got to be sheriff?
> D: By being a good citizen.
> Mrs C: David, what do good citizens do?
> D: They check up on others.
> Mrs C: Well that's not all they do.
> (Mrs C repeats the question for Frank)
> Frank: Good citizens obey the rules.
> Mrs C: That's right, Frank, good citizens obey the rules, no matter what they are.

I quote that exchange because it makes brutally explicit what for most of the time is conveyed by much more oblique means - tacit assumptions behind everyday discourse and practices which naturalize the way society works (familiar to us as the hidden curriculum). In its most extreme form the basic assumption subsumes these ideas:

(a) society as we know it is in a state of achieved perfection or if it is not it has never been bettered and never will be;
(b) we must play our cards right to ensure that no inferior form asserts itself;
(c) the 'rules' are in no way problematic;
(d) society is not a legitimate site for conflict since it is neutral and even-handed: the same rules apply for all.

By now you will be becoming impatient and wondering

what all this has got to do with writing. What about all those things we hear so much about, conferencing, redrafting, paragraphing, the use of journals, topic sentences, etc, etc? I hope some of you will have glimpsed a way of reading what I have been presenting which points in that direction. Mrs Caplow can be read in this way. A good writer (citizen) obeys the rules no matter what they are. And I don't just mean grammatical rules, spelling rules, etc but also discourse rules. One of the very few writers to have taken a socio-cultural view of writing, Gunther Kress, puts the matter gloomily when discussing genres, which we might call forms of discourse, kinds of writing etc. These different kinds of writing he says,

> .... are fixed, formalized and codified. Hence the learning of genres involves an increasing loss of creativity on the child's part and a subordination of the child's creative abilities to the demands of the genre. (p.11)

Or later in the book,

> .... just as there is a fixed number of sentence types so there exists a small fixed number of genres within any written tradition.

Now Kress is fully aware that kinds of writing are related to our social system but he never works out satisfactorily what that relationship is. The idea that writing is fixed, formalized and codified needs examining more closely. It is only partly so. There is not a fixed number of genres. (Note in passing that Kress does not reveal this magic number.) The point is that in both teaching and research we behave as though this is so. Moreover, the writing police - editors, employers, writers of school manuals and self-appointed controllers of other people's language - try to promote this world of fixed genres so that discourse itself in all its heterogeneity comes under the yoke of sets of rules. For all their intimidation they never quite succeed. Kress quite clearly perceives that learning to write is a form of socialization but he sees this in a very determinist way. According to him there is no escaping the iron rules.

Learning language is one of the highly developed rule

systems .... Learning genres .... represents the child's socialization into appropriate and accepted modes of organizing knowledge.
It is important to recognize that genres have this constraining effect and that they are conventions. (p.123)

So we are back to the rule of law and order with this important difference that Kress sees the source of that law and order and does not give it his stamp of approval. One interesting remark that he makes is that 'Other conventions can be imagined: indeed it is one of the main points of this book that children constantly invent their own modes of organizing and knowing which, however, do not become recognized as such but rather are categorized as errors.' It is my argument that to behave as though adult forms of writing are fixed and codified is to accept the messages which power delivers and to ignore what actually happens. The legitimized forms of writing are in fact constantly being eroded and undermined - and not just by children, just as are social norms, the family for instance. Writing is a site of conflict and ferocious play goes on within its boundaries. Old forms die out and new ones appear, others are in a state of flux. This is especially true if we stop thinking of typical prose and look at other forms. A few examples. First, consider obsolete and obsolescent forms. I take off the shelf beside me *A History of Leicester*, J. Throsby, 1791. It begins with the now obsolete sycophantic type of dedication complete with special layout.

To the
Right Honourable
George Townsend
Earl of the County of Leicester
Baron de Ferrars of Chartley
Lord Bourchier, Lorraine, Bassett and Compton

My Lord
    As the following sheets are the first published attempt at a regular history, the writer looks up to your Lordship in particular, as Patron to his labours. Your Lordship's supereminent station in the Antiquarian Society and your illustrious descent from the renowned Earl of Leicester show the

propriety of this address.

> He is,
> My Lord,
> with due deference
> John Throsby

Dedications are now either omitted entirely or go like this:

> For Boyd, Elizabeth, Greta without whom I could not have gotten on

Where is the code which specifies the rules governing that text? What is the fixed, formalized, codified set of rules for writing a philosophical work called 'A theory of history'? Would the rules (how many?) enable you to predict a passage of this type ?

> Once upon a time there was a man; we tell his story. Once upon a time there was a King, and he had three sons; we tell their miraculous stories. Once upon a time there was a hunter ....

But then Agnes Heller (1982) is not only a radical who writes but also someone who writes radically. And that is precisely my point. Of course there are many, many texts which we could group together and through analysis show to be governed by a code but -

(a) the rules are by no means as rigid as some would maintain (see the dogmatism of manual-writers and codifiers);
(b) the rules are constantly being abandoned, subverted, mocked, ignored, sometimes as a deliberate act of refusal, sometimes as intuitive innovation;
(c) the rules are tightest where very direct controls operate and a certain measure of power is in the hands of certain controllers - editors, employers, teachers who themselves came through a formation highly likely to make them eager rule-obeyers.

There is a long history to the evolution of this state of affairs. It has yet to be written. For the moment let us take a look at one corner of the field. *Harvard Educational Review*, which in practice is an enlightened journal and tolerates some diversity, informs its contributors that -

> All copy, including indented matter, footnotes and references, should be typed double-spaced and justified to the left margin only. The author should be identified only on the title page. Manuscripts should conform to the publication guidelines of the APA (for technical and research articles), the MLA Handbook (for theoretical, descriptive, or essay-style articles) or The Uniform System of Citation published by the Harvard Law Review (for legal articles). For general questions of style authors should consult The Chicago Manual of Style.

The recollection of lengthy transatlantic telephone calls reminds me just how seriously all this is taken. No wonder Enzensberger once remarked that we can see an attempt in our society to industrialize the mind. The attempt to drill students into conforming to certain supposed rules of discourse amounts to nothing less than the imposition of a code of unquestioning obedience. It turns them and us away from asking the important questions. Eagleton puts this very simply (*Introduction to Literary Theory*, 1983).

> The language of a legal document or scientific text may impress or even intimidate us because we do not see how the language got there in the first place. The text does not allow the reader to see how the facts it contains were selected, what was excluded, why these facts were organized in this particular way, what assumptions governed this process, what forms of work went into the making of the text and how all this might have been different.

In other words concealed beneath the surface of the most humdrum document which we would take for granted as a satisfactory not-to-be-tampered-with means for achieving its end, there is always a deeper social process at work. As students proceed through our schools and possibly into higher education they are unlikely to be encouraged to probe their own writing and that of others for the workings of this deeper social system.

One form a writing workshop might take would be the interrogation of a set of texts like these:

(a) Contrary to the impression we may have given in this column on 16th March, the Acme Thunder Railway Guards' Whistle marketed by Mailpost is made by J.Hudson and Co. (Whistles) Ltd., a British firm which has been manufacturing whistles for more than 130 years. The whistles offered by Mailpost are replicas.

(b) We are seeking to appoint an Officer in Charge to our Hostel for 20 emotionally and mentally distressed young adults at 15 Homerton Row, E.9. Applications are invited from mature, experienced men/women with qualities of management. The successful applicant ....

(c) Mum, Back at 11.30. Don't lock garden door. Leave caviar and champers in fridge. Chaz.

Jay Lemke in a fascinating paper [Thematic analysis: systems, structures, and strategies. *RS/SI*, Vol 3, 1982] asked a set of questions which might be applied to any text and which we in our turn might use to deconsecrate them.

- Who is doing what to whom in this text?
- How?
- What other texts and doings stand in what relevant relations for the meanings made and the acts performed by this text?
- What social systems are maintained or altered by what relations among the set of texts to which we may assign this one?
- What social interests annd their conflicting discourses are being served or contested in this text and through its intertextual relations?
- How does the text contribute to the maintenance and change of the linguistic system and the patterns of use of that system in the community?

To ask questions of this kind is, as Lemke says, ' to strengthen our ability to dispel the sense of givenness and inevitability .... and better arm us to contest them'. It might lead us to consider more carefully what we ask out students to write and how we respond to anything which is fresh and liberating.

We need to look at every form of writing as a specific form of social practice embedded in our social system and impregnated with its own social history. Our kind of scientific writing, for example, is the culmination of some three centuries of the development of science as an institution and is therefore the more likely to be thought to have attained a state of immutable perfection. When we have served an apprenticeship to any particular genre of writing we are not inevitably, inextricably enmeshed in its rule system. But greater awareness of that system and how it works can enable us to begin to free ourselves from some at least of its oppressive features.

You will know of course that over the last 15 years there has been a most significant shift in the research energies directed towards investigating language in schools. Writing has been discovered. We are in the process of redressing a strange imbalance (another piece of social history!) When we began our writing research at the University of London in 1966 there was available a whole library of work on reading whereas worthwhile work on writing consisted of a mere handful of books and monographs. We now have the results of large funded projects, a proliferation of models of the writing process, analyses of students' written texts, maps of functional diversity, blueprints for patterns of development and much more. A discriminating study of this literature can teach us a great deal. But in preparing this paper I set my face against reviewing this fresh material. Let me explain why. For all the insights and useful findings there has been a consistent failure to address the issues I have been exploring. There has been no attempt to question the goal (good writing? mature writing? competent writing? genre writing? etc.) Largely the goal(s) have been taken for granted no matter how elaborated they have become and the debate has focused on the route. To put it simply the unspoken proposition is, 'We know what good adult writing looks like: so let us research the best ways of attaining it'. If we know what kinds of acceptable language are used in our society then we can devise better ways of training students to use them. In terms of the old pieties this is part of the process of preparing children for society. Since there are many kinds of writing, we will need to establish priorities. Up pop the old favourites - the business letter, the job application, the essay. Should we add advertising copy? Kress is almost alone among those addressing writing in schools in pointing out,

> To become proficient in the genre one has to become absorbed of these contents [i.e. ideological and cognitive contents H.R.] and of the institution itself. Effective teaching of genres can make the individual into an efficiently intuitive and unreflective user of the genre. The genre and its meanings will come to dominate the individual .... and this is so whether he be scientist, bureaucrat or short story writer .... Is that we want? (p.125)

I do not hear that question being asked by most of those engaged currently on work on writing. I grumble once again at Kress's assumption that the more we are drawn into the system the more inevitably we accept its hidden agenda. The literate culture is full of examples of writers who conduct unceasing guerilla warfare against it. How, for example, do you write for an audience of educationists about writing? Easy. Follow this model.

> A common assumption shared by many rhetoricians is that the act of composing is linear. Gordon Rohman, for example, distinguishes three stages in the composing process: first the pre-writing, then the writing, and finally the re-writing. Pre-writing, like Aristotelian invention, is .... (Butturf and Sommers in Freedman and Pringle, 1980, p.99)

And so it continues in the same familiar vein. However, what do we find in the same volume in which one contribution after another obediently follows the tradition (as indeed does this paper for the most part!)? A contribution from Don Murray which begins by cheerfully defying the code, the rules and expectations.

> Emptiness. There will be no more words. Blackness. No, white without colour. Silence.
> I have not any words all day. It is late and I am tired in the bone. I sit on the edge of the bed, open the notebook, uncap the pen. Nothing.
> Or.
> Everything has gone well this morning. I wake from sleep, not dreams.

What follows is a set of juxtaposed stories, a collage, with none of the devices the manuals tell us are so necessary. A modernist text with the author's thumbprints all over it and the man unashamedly declaring himself.

All this leaves me in an uncomfortable position. Yes, the Don Murrays of this world, established and secure, may be able to thumb their noses at the conventions but their ways are scarcely a credible recipe for the teaching of writing. Suppose we do have an understanding that writing is an interlocking set of social practices shaped by the context of the society we live in. What are we expected to do about it? The students eventually have to get jobs, don't they? If they don't toe the line, they are finished. And how could we possibly change our teaching to accomodate the alternative view? The first part of my answer, as I have been suggesting, is that the Kress picture insufficiently accommodates the subtle diversity of possibilities within the written language and the promiscuity of genres. These possibilities are present from the moment a child starts to write. The real issue is whether we exploit these possibilities and help students to avoid being drawn inexorably into the embrace of house styles. The one theorist who sheds a helpful light on this matter is Bakhtin. He alone provides a base which shows how every act of writing can potentially break the code within which it is operating. In his book, *The Dialogic Imagination*, he argues that two forces are always at work in language use: he calls them centrifugal and centripetal. The centripetal describes all that which pulls us towards a centre of prescribed norms, genre conventions, discourse etiquettes etc. The counterforce is centrifugal which pulls away from the normative centre. Bakhtin says,

> Every utterance serves as a point where centrifugal as well as centripetal forces are brought to bear. The processes of centralization and decentralization, of unification and disunification, intersect in the utterance.

Linked with these concepts is Bakhtin's contrast between authoritative and internally persuasive discourse.

> .... in one the authoritative word (religious, political, moral, the word of the father, of adults, of teachers, etc.) that does not know internal persuasiveness; in the

other the internally persuasive word that is denied all privilege, backed up by no authority at all and is frequently not acknowledged in society (not by public opinion, nor by scholarly norms).

Authoritative discourse demands -

.... our unconditional allegiance - permits no play within its borders, no gradual or flexible transitions, no creative stylizing variants. It is indissolubly fused with authority. All is inertia and calcification.

Bakhtin's elaboration is much more complex than this but I have cited enough to show that his ideas open up new possibilities for students and teachers alike. We can see in every act of writing those two forces at work. We can never totally escape the centripetal pull: we cannot jump out of the language system and its practices. On the other hand we do not have to elevate that system into an object which has achieved perfection. On the contrary it is necessary to insist again and again on the need to disrupt the authoritative voice with the unheard voices of our students, to help them engage in the difficult struggle (so difficult for all of us) to articulate, develop, refine and advance their meanings as against the mere reproduction of the words of the textbook, the worksheet, the encyclopaedia and the guides. To insist on this involves squaring up to the oppressive power of authoritative language. Millions of notebooks, examination papers and 'essays' are crammed with words which are in essence no more than transcriptions, the forced labour of submission. The very least we can do is to emancipate ourselves from the notion that there is only one good and proper way and that way is quite rightly prescribed by others because they are paying the piper or because we have bowed before their assured authority without question. As against this what I find cheering is that many who would not subscribe to the views I have expressed or at any rate to the idiom in which I have expressed them know all that in their bones. They are the centrifugal teachers. (See the writing in *Beat not the poor desk* by Marie Ponsot and Rosemary Deen 1982.) In the early days of the Writing Project in the U.K. John Richmond (1986) set out shrewdly in diagrammatic form seven 'Key Ideas' about writing and placed them tellingly against 'what often happens in schools'. I should stress that he also extends an invitation to amend, add and disagree. He does not address the issue I have been trying to elaborate. Yet if we write it in as a subtext, each of the key ideas can be seen in sharper form. Let me try that with a few of them.

> **Writers As Assessors**
> The development of a critical sense, the ability to get outside of your own or someone else's product, to make judgements, is an essential half of the reflexivity between creation and criticism. Writers need it.

Agree heartily. But what is the platform from which the criticism is to be launched? Any well-indoctrinated students, including very young ones, may have internalized a set of criteria which will lead them to place their own efforts solely against the authoritative model. Are there binding rules for the structure of a story? Or a lab report? What kind of teaching emancipates students from that punishing form of self-criticism?

> **Collaboration**
> The process of interaction, conversation, mutual support and criticism grants orientation and critical space to the writer as well as the benefits of others' ideas.

This is better still. For here is the moment when the large social processes filter into everyday exchanges but also when the culture and values of the students have a chance to emerge - but only if teachers nurture and validate centrifugal moves. There is a huge discourse of experience which is largely censored out - collaboration is one way to let it in. It must be added that if what is being collaborated on is itself suspect (the imitation of a piece of inflated descriptive writing, for instance) it will contribute very little or nothing.

> **Development**
> All writers come from somewhere and are going towards somewhere as long as they keep writing. Going towards somewhere else does not necessarily mean somewhere good; some developments are blind alleys or red herrings.

Nearly but not quite. It is not so much a matter of blind

alleys or red herrings (I'm not sure what that's about). Some writers are slowly heading towards a facile capacity to churn out pieces which conform perfectly to available models.

In applying any of these key ideas it would help if we bore in mind Bakhtin's reminder - 'language is not a neutral medium that passes freely and easily into the private property of the speaker's intentions .... expropriating it, forcing it to submit to one's own intentions is a difficult and complicated process'.

'We never write on a blank page but always on one that has already been written on.' says de Certeau (p.43). To write is to engage with social history, the social history of discourse but it can never be the total history, only the writer's particular links with that history. What is pre-inscribed on the page is different for each one of us. Never to have encountered the classic folk tale or blank verse is to have these forms erased from the page. There is gain and loss. On the one hand the writer is released from the tyranny of the model and on the other is more limited in choice and support. As the pen moves and in crucial pauses the writer is making choice after choice powerfully affected by the already inscribed invisible texts. With each specific piece of writing the invisible consists of the matrices of particular genres, a selection of lexicon, formalities, mini-structures, stylistic devices and so on. What asserts its presence will be different if I am writing a fable, a pseudo-folk story, some notes for a lecture, a set of instructions, a letter to my wife. Indeed, one of the ways of forcing the writing to submit to my intentions is to call up the 'inappropriate' model or to mix one tradition with another. This is a possibility whatever the work in hand. But there is one mode which lends itself to this tactic more than any other - narrative. Of course we all know that there are profoundly established stereotypes but there are two properties of narrative which leave it open to the play of infinite possibilities:

(a) we inherit an enormous range of resources;
(b) within the text of any one narrative there is infinite space for play, juxtaposing strategies and tactics drawn from any kind of discourse.

Here is Helen, aged 11, demonstrating the use of these possibilities.

The Hero Howard

Howard was the city's most cowardly man. He had one ambition and that was to marry the King's daughter, Princess Victoria. She was a beautiful girl with silky brown hair. She said, 'Whoever kills Great Hadden, the fierce, fiery dragon, I will marry.'
On hearing this, Howard decided to kill the dragon. He went to the library and asked for books about killing dragons and marrying princesses. The librarian looked rather surprised and told him to go to the children's department, thinking he was looking for books for his children. He came out of the library with a big pile of fairy tales to read.
(Later in the story the librarian writes Howard a letter. It is couched in perfect bureaucratic prose.)

The play of language here consists of the intertwining of two sets of social meanings which have accreted around specific genres (folk-tales, realistic short stories, farcical tales, official letters, kinds of conversation) and by these means to coax a new meaning out of the text. Helen has successfully refused to make the forced march through enemy territory and has set off on a jaunty discourse journey of her own.

As a last step let me suggest, pursuing the possibilities of narrative, how all students from the youngest to the oldest might be helped to make that journey. My major current interest is the exploration, with the aid, inventiveness and illumination of a network of classroom teachers, of the processes and consequences of the re-telling of stories. I am not intending to report on that activity here but I would like to offer you an illustration drawn from it. John Scurr School (primary) is in the heart of the inner city. Two thirds of its pupils are Bangladeshi and speakers of Sylheti. It is a school where story-telling by the teachers occupies an unchallenged place in the curriculum and that includes bi-lingual story-telling which we have recently been scrutinizing. In a class which I now know quite well (10/11-year-olds) I told an Italian folk story, *The Land Where No One Ever Dies*. It is a subtle and ironic tale of time and death. I proposed that the children should re-tell the story in writing. My only suggestion was, 'Tell it which way you like. Change anything you like.' I watched the children with some misgiving as after a generous amount of time they had written very little, perhaps some 5 to 10 lines. With no prompting from me they promised they would finish before my next visit. Two weeks later I returned to do some more story-telling. Joe, the teacher, put a folder in my hands. It contained all the children's re-tellings. In them you can find dozens of ways in which they have shifted the genre, frequently by filling the story with contemporary dialogue. Most striking perhaps is the very shy little girl who changed the chief character of the story from the inevitable young man to a young woman who instead of setting out on her own takes the whole family with her!

Now let me shift the context. We are still in the inner city but this time in a class of fifteen-year-olds. There is a strong contingent of students of Caribbean origin and the rest are as ethnically diverse as they come. Here the teacher has designed a whole unit on re-telling which includes much discussion of ways in which stories can be changed. This unit is based on Greek legends, a surprise perhaps given the context. At one point she tells her very lyrical version of the Orpheus story. Here too the students are invited to re-tell in writing. And here too they move outwards from the told version using every possible ruse to shift it to their own telling, changing events, characters, language, dialogue, points of entry and exit, omitting and adding. (Since the presentation of this paper the teacher has published a book-length account of her work. See *And None of it Was Nonsense* by Betty Rosen, published by Mary Glasgow. The material on Orpheus can be found in Chap.11, pp.129-147.)

Narrative, but more especially re-telling, is a one way of wriggling out of the coils of the quasi-official written codes because it positively invites cunning. The story is given, established, approved. Within its confines it is possible while nodding agreement to defy it. Defy it to just the extent we wish. A nice paradox then appears in the ways we all operate. The beauty of re-telling is that while it appears to desert invention (the old rhetorical term) it lets it in by the back door. At the intimate level of the classroom a micro-culture of shared discourse can assert itself.

References

Bahktin, M.M. (1981), *The Dialogic Imagination*, University of Texas

Butturf, O.R. and Sommers, N.l. (1980), 'Placing revision in a reinvented rhetorical tradition' in A. Freedman and 1. Pringle (eds), *Reinventing the Rhetorical Tradition*, CCTE and L and S Books, University of Central Arkansas

de Certeau, M. (1984), *The Practice of Everyday Life*, University of California

Eagleton, T. (1983), *Introduction to Literary Theory*, Basil Blackwell

Giroux, H. (1983), *Theory and Resistance in Education*, Heinemann Educational

Goody, J. (1977), *The Domestication of The Savage Mind*, Cambridge University Press

Heath, S.B. (1983), *Ways With Words*, Cambridge University Press

Heller, A. (1982), *A Theory of History*, Routledge & Kegan Paul

Kress, G. (1982), *Learning To Write*, Routledge & Kegan Paul

Kress, G. (1989), 'Texture and meaning' in R. Andrews (ed.), *Narrative and Argument*, Open University

Lemke, J. (1982), 'Thematic analysis: systems, structures and strategies' in *RS/SI*, vol 3

Murray, D. (1980), 'The feel of writing - and teaching writing' in A. Freedman and I. Pringle (eds), *Reinventing the Rhetorical Tradition*, CCTE (see above, Butturf and Sommers)

Olsen, D.R. (1977), 'From utterance to text: the bias of language in speech and writing' in *Harvard Educational Review* 47 (3)

Ong, W. (1982), *Orality and Literacy*, Methuen

Ponsot, M. and Dean, R. (1982), *Beat not the Poor Desk*, Boynton

Reid, E (ed) (1987), *The Place of Genre in Learning: Current debates*, Deakin University

Richmond, J. (1986), *About Writing*, no. 2, Spring 1986 National Writing Project

Rosen, B. (1988), *And None of It was Nonsense*, Harper Collins

Rosen,.B (l988)*Shapers and Polishers*, Harper Collins

Throsby, J. (1791), *A History of Leicester*

Talk As Autobiography

Paper delivered in Toronto, May, 1991

(Readers who have read the stories at the beginning of this book will recognise what seem like snippets from them in this paper. In fact they're somewhat different. That's because the paper was presented before the oral stories were turned into written tales.)

Thereby always hangs a tale. For instance, the two-inch scar just below my left ankle which is sixty-two or sixty-three years old. Or the battered photo of my older brother Laurie in the uniform of the 11th Hussars who ran away from home when he was sixteen and who I never saw again. Or the story that explains how it was that I became a teacher even though when I was sixteen I was sure I was going to become a lawyer. These are tales (and at my age there are many, many of them) which are, to use Gorky's phrase, fragments of my autobiography. They are not very long and if I tell one of them yet again, it will usually be in the midst of a conversation. If I could bring them all together I would be content to say, 'There you are, that's me'. Which is what Jean-Jacques Rousseau said at the beginning of *The Confessions*. There's nothing special in that. Everyone has a similar repertoire, an invisible autobiography. We are at it all the time. So are our pupils even when their pasts amount to very few years.

The trouble is that, like most words of Greek origin

invented by the educated, autobiography is a heavy word. We didn't, it would seem, even have the word until shortly after 1800. Yet when we think of the kinds of activities meant by it we are comfortable enough. We've read an autobiography or two and probably quite a few novels which are written as though they are autobiographies and of course sometimes are. For instance:

> 'You must not tell anyone,' my mother said, 'what I am about to tell you. In China your father had a sister who killed herself. She jumped into the family well. We say that your father has all brothers because it is as if she had never been born ....   The Woman Warrior, Maxine Hong Kingston.

I suppose that if I asked you what sort of thing autobiography is, you'd answer, 'It's someone telling his/her life-story' which sounds like an ambitious project, not one a person would undertake lightly. Listen to the opening words of Rousseau's *Confessions*:

> I have resolved on an enterprise which has no precedents and which, once complete, will have no imitator. My purpose is to display to my kind a portrait in every way true to nature. The man I portray will be myself.

'Portrait' is a kind of metaphor, of course. *The Confessions* turns out to be a long story within which are dozens of other stories. Rousseau's claim to uniqueness at that time was certainly justified but only if we discount such things as journals, diaries, letters, traveller's tales and personal stories interpolated into almost any kind of work. We can go back as far as Bede's Ecclesiastical History and we find in the eighth century Bede writing about his religious and scholarly life in the monastery. And of course we have Pepys' seventeenth century diary. Nowadays we take for granted that everyone has a life story even if they never get round to telling it. Perhaps we do not notice how much of it they do tell when they just sit and chat. Nor do we notice how much the culture has taught them how to do it, how it licenses self-revelation. They do not learn this complex and delicate art from literature, linguists or psychology classes but in the very processes of talking and listening to one another. That is why we should shift our attention away from the portentous sense of autobiography in the printed tome to that verbal world where, I believe, such works have their roots (i.e. the day-to-day world of common interchange) but also where we would learn something important about all autobiographical activity and the role it plays in everyone's life. But it requires a special effort. Just as it is difficult to pay attention to the very air we breathe or to observe what makes up our culture, so it is difficult to notice what goes on in conversation. If we listen carefully to intimate, friendly, relaxed talk (or eavesdrop, I might almost say) or better still attend closely to tape and transcript of such talk, we shall always find that the participants offer each other moments of their pasts, recent or distant. They are not only saying 'This is how it was' and 'This is the way I am' but also 'This is the way the world goes'. Some conversations consist of almost nothing else: they are little anthologies about, let us say, domestic disasters, recollections of schooldays, holiday episodes, our children, incidents at work, inexplicable mysterious events and so on. We make these offerings as fully fledged stories or as very brief utterances. Take the former. We recognise the initiating signals:

That reminds me of the time ....
Did I ever tell you about ....

and usually we accord more than the average ration of space given to a speaker and surrender our turns as a small price to pay for what we expect to be a proper story. Context, of course, makes a huge difference. Suppose I tell my teacher friends how I came to leave a job unexpectedly and then I have to tell the same story when I am asked about it at a formal interview for the next job. Those would be rather different tellings and I think we can safely say that the second would be carefully censored and hedged about with much more verbal caution than the first. Though all stories of personal experience share underlying characteristics, there are important differences. They may be no more than the briefest intimation of past events:

I never questioned or challenged my parents' views until I was nineteen ....
That party was a real washout, a flop ....

At a different time and given more propitious circumstances, they might have blossomed into full stories. After all, I haven't told you the full story of the scar under my ankle or of my brother Laurie's photo. Or take this snippet:

A. Do you know that since I've lived here four kids have died in that damned canal?
B. Yeah. When I was twelve I fell in ....

But the conversation is about putting pressure on the local council to organise better safety precautions and it sweeps on, leaving only the trace of what might have been the full tale. Some other time perhaps. At the other pole is that repertoire of stories which, as far as I can tell, everyone has tucked away in the pouch. Given the right moment in the conversation - encouragement, provocation, rivalry, the need to establish identity, etc. - the fully-fledged personal experience story emerges. Or it may be that an episode which has never been put in words before will be trawled from memory and given an airing. By contrast, repertoires often contain stories which have been polished over many tellings, like the one I tell about visiting an old manor house in Devon. After looking over the house we settled down in a corner of the lawn to eat our lunch. Major what-ever-he-was came charging out and said, 'Do you usually eat your meals on other people's lawns?' and we crawled away: that was only the coup de grace after a series of devastating put-downs. Stories like that often achieve an almost canonical form and change very little from one telling to another, many wordings remaining intact, although there will always be some adjustments as we shall see later.

We can take it, then, that there is a spectrum of autobiographical talk, from a remark like:

I came to England when I was three years old

to a full version of how I sat an algebra exam and half-way through decided I couldn't pass. In despair I put my pen down and listened to a barrel organ playing a waltz I associated with my mother. Somehow soothed, I picked up my pen again .... Of course there's more to it than a simple continuum from short to long, for on any point on that continuum we can distinguish differences. Let me take the extremes.

A. The brief utterance: why is it brief?
i. It is brief because that's all the speaker wants to say at that moment.
ii. It is brief because that's all the speaker gets a chance to say.
iii. It is brief because the speaker hoped for encouragement which did not come.
iv. It is brief because the speaker is not yet ready to develop the story or is unsure about how to develop it. Perhaps memory has not thrown up the detail.

B. The fully-fledged story: why is it being told?
i. It is being told because it's a serious contribution to a discussion, an alternative to other ways of making a point, where opinions are being exchanged, explored, re-shaped.
ii. An anecdote can itself initiate a discussion, e.g. indignation events (a student tells a group how a teacher has unjustly accused him of cheating and not allowed him to defend himself. The others then launch into a discussion of the vagaries and mysteries of teacher behaviour).
iii. The story is being told in its own right, i.e. its only justification is that it is calculated to command full attention and interest. The implication is that 'you're going to enjoy this'. A sub-genre is when the whole group moves into the storytelling mode, e.g. hospital stories, supernatural episodes, dreams etc. That at any rate is the surface phenomenon. Such story sequences are often, in fact, alternative ways of conducting a discussion. We know that conversation involves the skilled art of turn-taking and a special form of this is turn-taking at storytelling.
iv. Those who have shared a significant set of experiences will engage in collective reminiscences e.g. those who were at school together ten or twenty years ago; parents and their now adult children looking back at their earlier shared life.
v. A story is told in response to some form of invitation, e.g. tell me what happened or tell them about the time when .... This, of course, could be sinister because some responses to invitations are made under the duress of interrogation.

To the best of my knowledge no one has made a thoroughgoing attempt to produce a taxonomy of the forms of autobiographical talk looked at linguistically, psychologically and socially. However, Sandra Stahl in three carefully worked papers has attempted to take an analytical look at stories of personal experience. I will not attempt to summarise them but I want simply to draw attention here to the two broad categories into which she divides those stories:

i. the self-oriented, in which the tellers emphasise their own involvement, their own self-image, the motives and values behind the actions.
ii. the other-oriented, in which the tellers underplay or eliminate entirely their own personal role. They become witnesses much more than participants.

That's just a two-category system along one dimension. For the rest, notice that all we have instead of a taxonomy is simply a collection of terms, some used by scholars, some by ordinary folk and some by both. Here's my collection - personal experience stories, oral personal narrative, autobiographical speech, chronicates, secular chronicates, true oral stories, recollections, reminiscences, eye-witness accounts, anecdotes, case histories, gossip, rumour. What most of these terms indicate is that there is a strong and diffuse folk-awareness of the mode.

To understand the personal experience narrative, it is necessary to say an all too brief word or two about narrative in general. There has been, as many of you will know, a huge surge of interest in narrative over the last twenty years which has gone far beyond literary criticism. A new discipline has been created, narratology, though it limits its territory very narrowly. Gerald Prince, a major exponent, tells us that it concerns itself with what all narratives have in common and what distinguishes them from other forms of discourse. What Prince's statement omits is a profound socio-psychological idea, namely that narrative is a major activity of the human mind. Or as some have said, a primary and irreducible form of human comprehension, an article in the constitution of human common sense, the central function or instance of the human mind. These are massive claims, aren't they? Those who say such things are not only talking about vast and renowned narratives like Tolstoy's *War and Peace*, Proust's *In Remembrance of Things Past* or

Gibbon's *Decline and Fall of the Roman Empire* but are also linking them to the sort of thing any one of us might say at any moment about which I was speaking earlier.

> - I couldn't get to sleep last night. There was a hell of a noise from cars in the street. So I went to the window ....
> - Sorry I couldn't get over last Tuesday. A miserable two inches of snow and the whole of this area came to a stand-still (from a Canadian in England!)

What embraces all narratives is what they reveal about the working of the human mind. For our purposes just now I shall give a very simple definition of narrative. Narrative is the representation in a text, written or spoken, of a sequence of interconnected events. We shall see that in order to produce or respond to that representation calls for complex thinking and verbalization. More of that later.

Side by side with feverish academic activity there has been the revival of storytelling. No need, I understand, to tell you that in Toronto. There are now professional storytellers; local virtuosi have been winkled out from their rural backwoods; there are storytelling clubs; there are storytelling festivals. Mostly the stories told are traditional but there are also occasions which elicit autobiography, in community projects, oral history sessions and the reservoir tapped by folklorists. Moreover, autobiography is often threaded into both the telling of and the listening to a traditional story.

So, from the renowned scholar in his study speculating about story grammar to an eighty-year-old remembering his first day at work there has developed a new world of narrative consciousness and narrative activity. However, as always happens when a new field opens up, the distribution of attention is very uneven. Autobiographical talk has until now received very little attention. Perhaps that is going to change because a scholar with a world reputation, Jerome Bruner, is making it the central object of study. I give a mere summary of his ideas on the subject, though they will appear in a forthcoming book. In 1986, in his book *Actual Minds, Possible Worlds* he signalled or registered a major shift in his interests as a psychologist and educationist. In it there is one chapter in particular entitled 'Two Modes of Thought' in which he sets out a radical view. The telling of stories, he maintains, is not merely a discourse choice we may make from time to time among all sorts of options but rather one of only two ways of telling and thinking. Here is the crucial passage:

> There are two modes of cognitive functioning, two modes of thought, each providing distinctive ways of ordering experience. The two (though complementary) are irreducible to one another. Efforts to ignore one at the expense of another inevitably fail to capture the rich diversity of human thought.

The two ways are paradigmatic (i.e. logical and scientific) and narrative. This is a bold, challenging, novel proposition and places narrative firmly in the cognitive domain, a way of ordering experience. To elaborate on this idea Bruner's analysis concentrates on the fiction story, though clearly he must have in mind also stories of personal experience. Now, although one would never have guessed it from his first sally into narrative, this is exactly the next move he made. He was good enough to send me the series of papers he had written . They are:

'Life as Narrative' (1987)
'The Narrative Construction of Reality' (1990)
'Self-Making and World-Making' (1990)
'Culture and Human Development' (1990)
'The Autobiographical Process' (forthcoming)

Moreover, we are promised a book (a collaboration with Susan Weisser) which will document his investigations, *Autobiography and the Construction of the Self*.

At the heart of Bruner's thinking on autobiographical stories is a challenge to us. For he says the way we know about the physical world is not the same as the way in which we develop and refine our knowledge of ourselves and others and the way in which we construct and represent human interaction. We learn about people and the social world differently from how we learn about things - how a car works or the structure of the atom. We do the former, he says, mainly narratively. That is the meaning of all those gossipy little stories which as our education proceeds are so frequently dismissed as a trivial, low-level activity which needs to be cured. We might almost say that in higher education the guiding precept is 'Forget the stories, learn to generalize, learn to be theoretical, be impersonal'. If Bruner is even half-way right then I think he is saying 'Sacrifice your autobiographical thinking and telling and you sacrifice a major form of learning'.

The next step Bruner takes is to test his speculations empirically by asking a number of people to tell their life stories in half an hour. You must seek out the details and dramatic surprises for yourselves. At the moment Bruner's conclusion runs like this:

> My life as a student of mind has taught me one incontrovertible lesson. Mind is never free of pre-commitment. There is no innocent eye, nor is there one that penetrates aboriginality. There are instead hypotheses, versions, expected scenarios. Our pre-commitment about the nature of life is that it is a story, some narrative, however incoherently put together.... the only life worth living is the well-examined one

That is just a whiff of the excitements to be found in Bruner. In the London Narrative Group we have tried to replicate Bruner's work with the half-hour life story. No one seems to have difficulty in taking it on, no matter what their age, education, kind of social life. But unlike Bruner's people, ours find it impossible to limit themselves to half an hour. My own victim, a twenty-nine-year-old used up the complete hour of tape and he had only reached the age of eighteen! 'That was the turning point,' he told me. 'What changed then?' I asked him. 'My parents told me that as I was eighteen I was now a man. I took them at their word and started to behave like one.' We have also noticed that some of our people go about the task in a different way from Bruner's. They do not deliver their half-hour life histories in a single trajectory. They offer them more as objective testimony, evidence of how life was or as dredged up separate memory images. This is what Sandra Stahl calls other-directed. An old lady in her nineties, totally compos mentis, remembers a whole universe of social life but she keeps her own feelings very much in the background.

Bruner until now has not turned his attention to those fleeting autobiographical glints which illuminate every conversation, to which I have already referred and which I see as the starting point for all autobiographical activity. We have to speculate about what precisely it is in interaction which fans a small red glow into the blaze of a full story. Certainly the teller must chance his/her arm and rely on an intuition that the story will either clinch an argument or be savoured as verbal art, as oral literature. What sort of judgement was involved when my son, returning from field work on a coral reef in the Indian Ocean told us about the Moray eel. He had been snorkelling along a reef and prising off small pieces of coral with a crowbar. At one point he said he felt a sudden and juddering clonk on the crowbar. It was a snapping bite from the Moray eel which lurks in the fissures of the coral. A bite from it could take your arm off. Why was it he chose to tell that little tale when he came back and not in one of his many storyful letters?

Reminiscences are about remembering but the literature on narrative pays little attention to the role of memory. Prince's *Dictionary of Narratology* does not even have an entry under memory. It takes a James Britton to remind us that:

> going over past events must occupy us for a great deal of our spare time .... Memory, as we usually think of it, takes a narrative form.

Memory is implicated in personal experience stories in different ways. We begin with how we actually experience events and the recall of those events in short-term memory. That is, what we remember and how we remember it, let us say an hour later. And then there is the long-term memory, possibly decades after the event. Further, there is the construction of the memory in words, the telling of the memory. Lastly, in order to tell it we must remember the appropriate forms for telling which we have learned from others since our earliest years as surely as we have learned 'Once upon a time ....' The goals and intentions of many remarkably perceptive scholars, Genette, Chapman, Prince and others, do not include considerations which any teacher, indeed any participant, would take for granted - the motives of the teller (why is she telling me this?), what is the personal point of a story (was the tale of the Moray eel to show the dangers to be faced when working on the reef? Was it a sort of rite of passage?); more broadly, what does a story tell us about the teller? What do I now know about the teller which I didn't know before? Our interest in the person who is engaged in the act of remembering includes an interest in how that person's memory is working. For James Britton, autobiographical stories are first and foremost an act of the remembering mind. For me that means a mind ceaselessly reviewing the past to confront its riddles, to rework it, to resavour it, to celebrate it, to mourn it. In a word, to wrest a huge array of meanings from it. Raw events and actions, lingering images of places and people are transformed by memory into causes, motives, consequences and point.

The story of personal experience might almost be called the making of memory. We do not easily perceive that such a story cannot be a straight reproduction of past events, the plain unvarnished truth, as we say. We do not in spite of our strong belief that this is often so, re-live an experience. We cannot put on a re-run of the past. We have to create beginnings, select some details and ignore others, we must adapt to an audience and our telling is likely to be suffused with our present feelings. To tell the tale of how I didn't become a lawyer I must confront what was a non-stop flow of events and cut right into them to create a beginning, which need not be either an event or an action but simply a way of signalling that I am about to begin a story. The choice is mine. I could make a general comment on my life and on the theme of the story.

> You know how it is. I was sixteen and didn't have the faintest idea about what I would do or what I wanted to be. That is until Cousin Leslie paid us one of his rare condescending visits.

This is my first step in the demarcation of the events of my story, where I choose to put the entrance door. I must then proceed with my construction work so that what was inchoate, interpenetrated with what now seems to me irrelevant other events, is now given shape by a process of selection, by systems of emphasis, silences, evaluations, indications of causality, cunning digressions, reflections, accommodation of the listener. I may even take to invention. For example:

> so I picked up the phone. I was nervous, very nervous. 'Can I speak to Mr Sunshine, please?' They put me through. 'It's me, Leslie,Harold. My exams .... You know, well.... I passed!'

Now that memory, which I would swear to, is that I DID phone cousin Leslie from the call box outside the Sussex Laundry in New Road. I am equally certain that I gave him my exam results on which I thought, wrongly as it turned out, my future as a lawyer depended. But how could I remember at fifty-four years distance the actual words I spoke over the telephone? So the words I use telling the story are fabricated but very faithful to the events.

The boundary must finally be drawn with an ending which in reality was no such thing. Life, as we keep telling ourselves, must go on. Stories must end and end appropriately. The endingness of the final event in some way or another must constitute a comment and be composed.

> So I stood there waiting, waiting for the silence at the other end of the line to be broken. Nothing. Was he still there? So I said again, 'Leslie, I passed; I passed my Matric.' 'Ah, your Matric .... You did, did you? Congratulations.'

And he put down the phone.

In telling that story it's not only my memory of the events and their penumbras on which I draw but also on an infinity of models learnt unawares from those around me.

Because we develop a rich experience of hearing and recounting stories from life, we see one experience rather than another as being story-worthy. So the experience of changing a tyre without the least difficulty is not worth the telling. But suppose everything goes wrong: the spare is flat, I've mislaid the pump, I've broken a spanner and cut my finger, it rains throughout. My son comes out and, in the midst of my despair and anger, asks 'Why didn't you say you were changing a tyre? I'd have given you a hand'. I do not kill him. Now we have the possibility of a story. Despite what I have already said about beginnings and endings they are to some extent naturalized in the culture and are therefore clearly perceived as ready to be appropriated. Football matches begin with the kick-off and end with the final whistle. But a storyteller who might be one of the players need not be constrained by that pattern. He might begin with a quarrel in the dressing-room or his thoughts while packing his kit. It would be interesting to know more about those sets of events in which we perceive a compelling story apparently ready-made.

A further point about the composing process. A personal story about the distant past is subject to important changes over the years. I told a story about how my grandfather, a tailor all his life, handled and tested a piece of cloth from which he was going to make me a suit. I first told the story, I imagine, because it was an intimate experience of the skills of a craftsman - judgement and expertise in action. Donkeys years later the story changed fairly subtly because of the frequent and increasing evocation of my grandfather in my thoughts as an object of admiration and love. The distant memory is filtered through intervening relevant experience which is also represented in my memory; then and now are indissolubly fused together.

De Certeau speaks of 'the sly, gossipy practices of story-telling'.

> .... In these stories all the features of the art of memory can be detected .... The art of daily life can be witnessed in the tales told about it.

So memory is not simply a function of the mind, it is also an art. The oral storyteller is not like the ghosts who haunt the shadows behind written texts, those we call authors. Their presentations are communicative acts performed in the presence of known or knowable people. It is quite impossible to participate in storytelling and not be intensely aware of who is telling, who is listening and, very often, the shared history of the group. The invitation to share a memory is usually a convivial act or, at the very least, the invitation to some kind of assent. To share a memory with someone you know is to advance your relationship even if it is only by the tiniest step.

The working of memory into a story is not by itself enough, for orality demands performance. The storyteller has to accept a certain responsibility for the display of culturally-learned skills - use of voice, variations in speed, pitch, volume, voice quality, intonation and silence. Add to that facial expression, gesture, direction of gaze and all kinds of body language.

Listeners are ruthless judges. They not only weigh what they are told as it might be a story of courage or cowardice, but also the performance itself, the level of skills of the storyteller, the totality of his or her expressive powers. As Bauman puts it:

> performance thus calls forth special attention to and heightened awareness of both the act of expression and the performer.

However, should the teller exert too much effort in drawing attention to the performance rather than the tale ('look how good I am at this') we resist, shift uneasily and become a little embarrassed. He's going over the top, we say.

Personal story-telling then calls for an active, exacting attention both to the world and the word, the very kind of attention which should be at the heart of all learning. In the classroom an invitation to tell that kind of story should be seen as a call for attention of a very high order which will also dig deep into the linguistic resources of the narrator. Ask yourselves now what it is which is most likely to lure someone into offering a story of personal experience. For there are, after all, hazards in such revelations. Such a one is a show-off. The classroom is not thought to be the appropriate place: it's before total strangers or it's a particular cultural milieu which does not approve of such things. But if we know what enables a teller nimbly to elude such frosty condemnation then we have in our possession a powerful intimation of how to foster such stories in the classroom. Autobiographical storytelling belongs with trust, informality and conviviality and most easily comes into its own when people are comfortable with each other and do not feel constrained to be on their best behaviour. It not only emerges from a sense of ease but helps to create it. It confirms and extends social relationships - in the renewal of acquaintanceships, in those precious intervals on the job, at street corners, on long journeys, where ever knots of people gather together to become spectators of their own lives, uncensored by social anxiety. Memories exchanged on these occasions not only emerge from our own pasts but from the pasts told by others which have become available for retelling by us. Grandma's stories are also our stories. To make a space for students to tell their personal stories is above all to affirm the worth of their own culture and at the same time to enable them to make discoveries about it.

It has been a hard struggle over the years to convince others that common-or-garden talk, everyday, messy, interminable chatter, easily engaged in by everyone, navvies as well as Nobel Prize Winners, needed to be given full scope. The battle is far from won. We need, nevertheless, to extend the argument and to create an awareness of the significance of the anecdotal tissue of conversation. Bauman, after a detailed analysis of different kinds of Texan storytellers, says:

> When one looks at the social practices by which social life is accomplished, one finds with surprising frequency people telling stories to each other as a means of giving cognitive coherence to experience, constructing and negotiating social identity; investing the experiential landscape with moral significance .... Narrative here is not merely a reflection of the culture .... but is constitutive of social life.

Bauman only makes these strong claims after his analysis of the stories. We are all familiar with the claims made for the value of studying works of fiction. I think it makes good sense to see in both activities some of the same forces at work. Indeed, fiction writers have always drawn on the resources of oral personal recollection. A strong thread has always linked them together. Here, for example, is a snippet from my most recent novel reading:

> ....My father, as well as being a superstitious man, had a knack for telling stories. Made up stories; soothing stories; warning stories; stories with a moral or no point at all; believable stories and unbelievable stories; stories which were neither one thing or another. It was a knack which ran in the family.
> Graham Swift, *Waterland*

The power of oral storytelling which novelists plunder so freely derives from the human disposition to narratise experience using its own unique methods to create a cognitive, emotional, moral, social world.

So personal stories in all their forms could be said to be a kind of self-made curriculum. To take one simple anecdote by a child and invest it with such huge potential would be to invite ridicule but it is not the single isolated tale we must examine. It is the intricate web of narratives. Autobiographical stories, both in and out of school, are best regarded as a set of social practices which belong inside the larger set of narratives in general. They should find an honourable place in the narrative culture of the classroom.

References

Bauman, R. (1986) *Story, Performance and Event*, Cambridge University Press

Britton, J. (1970) *Language and Learning*, Allen Lane and Penguin Press

Bruner, J. (1986)*Actual Minds, Possible Worlds*, Harvard Univ Press

Bruner, J. and Weisser, S. (forthcoming) *Autobiography and the Construction of the Self*, Harvard Univ Press

de Certeau, M. (1980) 'On the oppositional practices of everyday life', *Social Texts*, 1 (3)

Chapman, S. (1978) *Story and Discourse*, Cornell Univ Press

Kingston, Maxine Hong (1975) *The Woman Warrior*, Vintage Books

Genette, G. (1980) *Narrative Discourse*, Basil Blackwell

Prince, G. (1988) *Dictionary of Narratology* Scolar Press

Rousseau J-J. (1781) *The Confessions*, trans. Cohen, J.X. (1953) Penguin Books

Stahl, Sandra (1977a) 'The oral personal narrative in its generic context' in *Fabula*, 18

(1977b) 'The personal narrative as folklore' in *Journal of the Folklore Institute* Vol X1V, No 1 - 2

(1983) 'Personal experience stories as folklore' in *Handbook of American Folklore*, Indiana University Press

Swift, G. (1980) *Waterland*, Picador

We Are Our Stories

Oral tradition encompasses all kinds of stories from riddles and jokes to folk-stories and legends. In a living tradition, all these can be valued and have their place. But what happens in societies where folktales and myths are rarely told?

Stories are everywhere: lined up on bookshelves (we call them novels), on television, in the theatre, in the cinema. All over the world in every culture there are traditional tales, thousands and thousands of them, retold again and again, reworked, transformed and changed. Story jokes travel at great speed from place to place. Listen in to any group of people chatting in a relaxed, intimate way and you will hear another kind of story - the story of personal experience or the story of hearsay. And so on and so on.

As different as they all are, we call them all stories. In some intuitive way we know that *Great Expectations* is in certain important respects the same in kind as *Cinderella*, or the one about the dog who went into a pub and ordered a beer, or my wife telling about the time when she took a moose skull wrapped in brown paper through Canadian customs. Stories are as common as dirt and therefore easily dismissed or at any rate not taken very seriously. There was a time when novel reading was thought of as a trivial activity fit only for light-headed young ladies. Stories are suitable for little children, we think, but in due course they will get round to more serious and important uses of language. Oral stories, the kind we find ourselves telling all the time (what happened to us this morning, last week, last year, when I was little), are so much part of the fabric of our everyday lives that, just like our conversation, gossip and chatter, we are not likely to think of them as very significant or important. Yet that's where storytelling begins and the very fact that we do so much of it points to its importance.

So let's take a closer look. First, let's notice that: relating the simplest anecdote is quite a complex business, requiring the mind to be fully active and creative. I could tell you the story about how, many years ago, my son and I were canoeing in the pouring rain on a tiny river on the Welsh Border, dressed in shorts and plastic bags, and how we frightened the life out of some villagers as we appeared suddenly from behind a hedge. Where does that story begin? Nowhere. Stories don't begin. We make them begin. We decide to start here rather than there. I could, for instance, start with the two of us staring out of the tent into the rain or with the sound of the Landrover coming up the farm lane with the canoe or in a hundred other ways.

The same applies to endings. Our lives just go on happening. They can't stop and say they'll start another story tomorrow. But in stories we, the storytellers, make endings.

- And I never saw him again.

- She went over to him, spat into his face and slowly walked out of the room.

- 'I can't speak German', I lied.

Between the beginning and the ending we choose to mention this, but not that, to digress for a few moments perhaps, to describe something or someone, to put in dialogue or compress it into a few phrases ('an argument broke out'), all the time selecting, sorting, ordering. It happens that my son has told the story of that canoe trip in a published poem. It's totally different from the way I would tell it. I keep wanting to say, 'But you left out the bit where ....' Of course he didn't leave it out. He was telling a different story. What all this choosing, selecting, omitting, shaping, amounts to is that these are the ways in which we make our stories meaningful. So it turns out that even our most gossipy, apparently trivial stories are ways of making meaning of our lives. Stories make organised sense out of very chaotic experiences. The process of constructing them is first and foremost a process we need to use for ourselves. After all, there are many stories we tell which never see the light of day.

We tell countless numbers of them to ourselves in our heads. Good stories do not make sense because they have a tidy hidden moral or because you can summarize their meaning neatly in a sentence. Meaning is distributed right through them, though we may feel that one meaning is more dominant than others.

However, there's much more to it than that. After all, we do tell our stories to others. We invite them to agree to our meanings. So storytelling is a basic form of communicating meaning. Many of the devices of storytellers (suspense is the one most often mentioned) are part of the act of seduction of the audience so that their attention is won for the real point and purpose of the tale. Every personal anecdote is a fragment of autobiography and to set about a full autobiography is to propose a meaning of life itself, to offer it to others. To engage intimately with others is to invite their stories, for it is via our stories that we present ourselves to each other. It is an interesting feature of personal storytelling that it usually sets in motion a sequence of stories. Tell a hospital story and you will provoke others, just as jokes beget jokes. If you analyse a sequence of this kind you will almost always discover that, far from being a random collection, they constitute an endeavour to reach a collective understanding of some important theme like fear, courage, loss, or eccentricity.

So then, all storytelling is an essential part of the functioning of the human mind. It is a major means of thinking and communicating our thoughts. That is why room must always be found for it in schools, for pupils of all ages, and why adults will listen entranced to old folktales. Many people would be surprised to learn that scholars of many different kinds, psychologists, linguists, sociologists, literary theorists, anthropologists, theologians, historians and folklorists, have all insisted that narrative is not an optional extra - froth on the surface of human behaviour - but 'the central function or instance of the human mind' (Frederic Jameson). Richard Bauman, who has studied both folkstories and personal tales, has come to the conclusion that an essential feature of managing our social lives is 'people telling stories to each other as a means of giving cognitive and emotional coherence to experience, constructing and negotiating social identity .... investing the experiential landscape with moral significance.' Not only do we have storytelling minds but we become social beings through storytelling. It is good to be reminded that not only the great novels but modest little tales can lay claim to profound functions. Great debate has waged for millennia on what constitutes the essence of being human. We can now propose as a candidate the disposition to narrate experience.

I have deliberately started at the humblest end of the narrative spectrum - the oral personal tale, but I want to move along it to take in traditional tales of all kinds, not as we find them in books but as they are retold by storytellers. We can notice in passing that there has been a vigorous revival of public storytelling, which you might think wouldn't stand a chance against the glamour of TV and cinema. I invite readers to work out why this is. Meanwhile we can consider why the spoken story has such power. Compare reading a folktale in one of the many magnificent collections now available with a telling of the same story. You would soon notice that all tellers make the story their own. They are not mesmerised by the original but take a path somewhere between being faithful to it and adapting it to their own sense of the story's meaning. Even another telling by the same teller is different, for the time and place change and the audience changes and the teller subtly adjusts to the mood and context of the moment, affected by visible reactions in the audience. Storytellers have available to them a repertoire of effects which writers, poor folk, do not possess - the tone of voice, the variations of pitch, pace, volume, the use of silence and body language. So the written version (these days we mostly encounter folktales in written form) is utterly transmogrified by the fact that it becomes a performance, not in the theatrical sense but rather as a direct doing and making and a collaboration with listeners. Thus the traditional tale is constantly being renewed and refreshed .

With the traditional tale we enter the realm of fiction, fantasy and magic, of talking beasts, magic rings, little people, of play with the passing of time, cleverness where it's least expected, tricks and riddles. Have we left the world of experience behind? Not a bit. For it is a feature of our humanness that we can not only represent experience directly but also work on the representation and thus deal with experience obliquely. A fiction story tells of events which, however improbable, are spoken of as though they actually occurred. The folktale, worked over and polished by generations of tellers, embodies communal ways of making sense of experience, operating through symbolic fictions. I have recently retold the Irish folk story about an osier cutter who, sadly, cannot tell stories. He is magically whisked away to a wake where, in spite of his protests about his incompetence, he plays the fiddle superbly, becomes a dignified officiating priest at a mass, and carries out a skilful and improbable piece of surgery. When he returns he has now, of course, a wonderful story to tell. He has become a storyteller. All the major episodes of the story are symbols of the human experience of diffidence and confidence.

We are beginning to discover that the act of storytelling raises the level of the language of the storyteller. Storytellers display a competence and power which is not present in their other uses of language. Charles Parker, who collaborated in those famous Radio Ballads like 'Singing the Fishing' and 'John Axon', always used to stress that the working class speakers whom he taped telling stories did so with amazing eloquence. Teachers are finding that students retelling stories are far more inventive and creative than when they are asked to 'make one up'. We need to understand this more fully. But it seems that the teller, no longer burdened with the need to invent the basic elements, is free to allow the imagination to play inventively. Surprising dormant resources come into action. A stereotypical character takes on a particular idiom and voice, a new episode is introduced, or an old one elaborated. This is the very opposite of repeating a rote-learned story. Retelling is a creative act.

A final word. Stories live off stories. Of all the genres learned through language, that is to say, ways of saying things - how to set out an argument, compose a letter of complaint, propose a toast, offer an explanation - narrative is the genre we are most comfortable with. From a very early age we gather a rich experience of stories and we learn more and more how they work, their methods and devices. So in our tellings, without our realising it, we use this hidden repertoire. We have a much more limited experience of the other genres but in storytelling we are comfortably at home. We are all storytellers, if only we are given the chance.

The Autobiographical Impulse

To begin somewhat autobiographically: in April of this year I was preparing a paper for the National Association for the Teaching of English and was casting about for a short exemplar of my opening point. I think I found it. I want to return to it now because I think my nugget contained more than I realized at the time.

Some time last year I found myself immersed in three very long mimeographed volumes by Dell Hymes[1]. He had pushed them into my hands with typical generosity when he noticed that I was ploughing my way through them in his outer office at the University of Pennsylvania. They constituted a vast elaboration of the now very familiar notion of communicative competence, and it could be described as an unremitting polemic against Chomsky's concept of competence. I did not find it an easy read. It was both dense and microscopic, pursuing its argument through every possible theoretical twist and turn; every concept was subjected to critical scrutiny. It was a kind of intellectual war of attrition. However, I persisted over several days for all the reasons you can guess at. For as they used to say in my family - draughts is draughts and chess is chess and there's no point in getting the two confused. I reached a point in the argument where Dell Hymes, having taken us step by step through a demonstration of the inadequacy of Chomsky's model, says with seductive simplicity, '.... a fair request would be to do better.' What happened next? Just this. I cite the text verbatim (Hymes 1973:1415):

Let me mention here Mrs. Blanche Tohet, who in the

summer of 1951 had David and Kay French and myself wait for a story until she had finished fixing eels. A tub of them had been caught the night before near Oregon City. Each had to be slit, the white cord within removed, and the spread skin cut in each of its four corners, held apart by sticks. The lot were then strung up on a line between poles, like so many shrunken infants' overalls, to dry. Mrs. Tohet stepped back, hands on hips, looking at the line of eels, and said: 'Ain't that beautiful!' (The sentence in its setting has been a touchstone for aesthetic theory for me ever since.) All then went in, and she told the story of Skunk, when his musk sac was stolen and carried down river, how he travelled down river in search of his 'golden thing,' asking each shrub, plant and tree in turn, and being answered civilly or curtly; how down the river he found boys playing shinny-ball with his sac, entered the game, got to the 'ball', popped it back in, and headed back up river, how, returning, he rewarded and punished, appointing those that had been nice to a useful role for the people who were soon to come into the land, denying usefulness to those who had been rude. All this in detail, with voices for different actors, gestures for the actions, and always, animation. For that as people will be glad to tell you, is what makes a good narrator: the ability to make the story come alive, to involve you as in a play. Despite the efforts of white schools and churches, there are people in whom such style lives today. Knowing them, it is impossible to think of them just as tacit grammarians; each is a voice.

For me that passage was much more than a respite or rest in the onward march of academic prose. It brought into the sharpest focus some key questions about narrative in general and autobiographical narrative in particular. What impulse drives a world-renowned scholar at the critical shift in his text, at its pivot or fulcrum, to scan his own past, to demand imperatively from it the recall of a few hours of experience, and cast them into this story about a story? How can he justify chatter about fixing eels amidst the interwoven propositions and abstractions of the rest of the text? It must be a reminder to us that his vast erudition is a superstructure erected on and motivated by meanings which had their beginnings and verifications in a past rich with encounters of this kind. I can do no more than surmise that in the process of the construction of many kinds of texts, spoken and written, the memories of the past are in constant play flashing beneath the still surface like gleaming fish in a still lake. We could enlarge Vygotsky's notion of the subtext of every utterance to include this clandestine presence of memory. This dramatic shift in rhetoric in Dell Hymes declares that the autobiographer locked away in a closet is for an instant coming out to propose another way of meaning and to recruit its persuasive power. Narrative, Chambers (1984) insists, is about desire and seduction. And autobiography permeates the seductive strategies of ordinary people. They are always at it with their damned anecdotes and what an impatient nineteenth century judge once called their 'dangerous confabulations.'

Hymes begins with an intriguing phrase to handle his transition, 'Let me mention here . . .' It is the storyteller's throwaway guile which advertises as a parenthesis what turns out to.be a central and bold effort to enlist your assent. The whole business of fixing eels could be written off as mere embroidery or even cheap bait. I think not. To tell the tale of one's own experiences is to trust what memory offers not in the sense of indiscriminate use of what it transmits but rather in rendering oneself hospitable to surprises both in the *what* and in the *how*. If Hymes is right and each one is a voice, it is a voice coming from a situated person. This kind of autobiography is memory verbalized into art - common, popular, unprivileged - that is to say, without a sanctioned locus in time and space. It marshals the ruses of discourse. Mrs Tohet's story, for all I know, may already have figured in a collection of folk-tales, where it would sit bereft of voice, bereft of the story of one particular telling.

We are looking at the story of a story. This is by no means a rare feature of autobiographical speech. It not only provokes responses in the same mode, chains of narrative, but provokes other tales in the teller. If we tell of other people, we recollect too the tales they told.

Memory again. We remember what others tell us they remember. That familiar device of narrative fiction, the story-within-the-story, has like so much else been borrowed from the oral story teller. Take the opening of Eco's *Name of the Rose (1983)*. We are to suppose that we are hearing a diligent contemporary scholar pursuing a manuscript across Europe which turns out to be the autobiography of a medieval monk and constitutes the main text of the novel. Thus we begin with the contemporary scholar's tale:

> ....as I was browsing among the bookshelves of a little antiquarian bookseller on Comentes ....I came upon a little work by Milos Temsvar...

And the tale of the monk begins:

> I prepare to leave on parchment my testimony as to the wondrous and terrible events that I happened to observe in my youth.

From a lifetime spent in the study of American Indian languages, Hymes has plucked this single instance. It comes with these components,

1. the eel-fixing
2. Mrs. Tohet's traditional tale; more exactly a stylized summary (a sequence of 'how, ...how ....etc.'), which omits the represented speech of the actors
3. a coda which shifts back to a non-narrative model in which Hymes makes clear his motive for telling the story but with a certain mockery ('It's impossible to think of them as tacit Grammarians') which never figures in his main text.

Thus the whole of this three-layered narration is intended to give power to his argument and general theme. And that is just how it is with us when spontaneous autobiography is inserted into the flow of conversation. Mrs. Tohet herself has no such readily construed designs on us. She is handing on from her culture a composition of events in such a manner that it constitutes 'an experimentation with life' and moral weight is enfolded in the tale. Here you might say that we have arrived at the opposite of autobiographical narrative. But that would be too easy. Though she is retelling a traditional tale which belongs with countless others, in its composition she imposes on it, literally and metaphorically, her own intonation, which is only another way of saying that her own experience makes its unique contribution to the communal one. A reanimator must not refuse her own learned life. This is not to propose that her tale is autobiographical; but I *do* want to suggest at this point no more than that autobiography is not easily tidied away into its most recognizable forms nor are our autobiographical moments simply microversions or primitive versions of the classic volumes of Gorki, Boswell or Rousseau[2].

Let me put alongside Hymes an analogue taken from a very animated spontaneous conversation. The occasion, to put it briefly, is a small - gathering of five people in an Afro-Caribbean club, four of them black, one a white researcher, David Sutcliffe. They are discussing their feelings about and attitudes towards white people. One of them, Miriam, a night-shift worker, at one point dominates the discussion.

> Now I've got five children, all born here, between the ages of 18 1/2 and 23. I've got three sons. And I would rather see them come through my door with a coloured girl. Admittedly, a whole lot of coloured girls born in England, they are only coloured outside. They are everything white like you people. They've got white minds. But I would still prefer that colour coming through my door.

We move through (a) autobiographical data - which establishes her speaking rights (compare Dell Hymes locating himself with his friends outside Oregon City), (b) explicit statement of attitude (which Hymes held back to the end), (c) analysis, (d) restatement of attitude ('coloured on the outside') - in stronger form.

The discussion then becomes noisy and heated as the group members try to decide whether they too are prejudiced. At this point Miriam intervenes again with, 'Well, there's a lot you could say about this sort of thing' which turns out to be a signal that she is about to capture conversational space. There follows what constitutes by far the longest turn in the whole lengthy discussion. The discussion itself is the equivalent of Hymes's general text. It surrounds this narrative moment.

> M: Well, there's a lot you could say about this sort of thing. Because, I mean, for instance, this, em, boy who seems to be very unlucky with his chosen white girl,

he's been going out with a girl, an English girl, for three years. He's been going to the girl's parents' home and they accept him.

Oh well it was alright - they were only young But when they got to eighteen ....of course I didn't even care to know the parents, did I? (ironic?). When they got to eighteen, one morning there was a knock on my door, (I had) just got into bed. And, mm, by the time I got downstairs, there was this woman turning back from the door. So I called to her and she turned back. And she introduced herself. She was of course my son's girlfriend's mother. And she called to get to know me, because she didn't know me after going out with ....her daughter going out with my son for three years. She just lived round the corner to me anyway. And what she called to say to me: (mimics) 'Did Andy tell you anything this morning?' I said: 'Anything about what?' Well I was at work the night before, and when I got home Boy had gone to work. So I said no. And she was crying tears, and she said: 'Well, we had such a row at home last night because my husband and I, we just can't get on with each other any more. Because mm - my husband is annoyed with our daughter going out with your son. Because they are getting older and they might decide to get married. And if they have children the children are going to be half-castes.' I say (hard voice) 'And you wait three years to say that? You didn't see what colour my son was when he was coming to your home over three years?! And if they have children and they don't want half-caste children - I say, 'Listen love, your daughter is going to have them, and you don't want them - I don't want them either (laughter). I've already warned my son not to come home pregnant.' (laughter)

I: (over the din): I think it's on both sides. Now we tell them at work. 'You are prejudiced, I am prejudiced.'

The whole of that would bear closer analysis. I must confine myself to a few points:

1. Miriam's conversational move shifts to her own life story which she trusts as a powerful form of argument.
2. It incorporates a fragment of the other woman's life story (I'll call it tip-of-the-iceberg autobiographical speech), 'we had such a row at home last night.'
3. To sustain the invasion of conversational space Miriam must deploy the ruses of the storyteller or forfeit it - thus her distribution of irony, especially in dialogue. But above all to maintain shape, a shape that has to be generated in the very act of utterance. The triumphal final joke seals the ending.
4. Unlike the momentary (but not insignificant) self-reference like:
> But my kids are English by birth because they were born in King Street Hospital and Paul was born in Whippendale Road - you can't get more bloody English than that.

when Miriam says, 'one morning there was a knock at my door,' the group will hear that as an announcement of the probability that a complete story is to follow and their listening posture will change accordingly.

To invoke autobiography is to take chances. One problem is how to avoid yet another excursion into liberal individualism. Another is how to avoid using autobiography as mere case history fodder and nothing more. There is the difficulty too that, in a sense, all utterances in day-to-day conversation, however generated, however self-protective, however deceitful, however self-censored, constitute, as Goffman showed, a presentation of the self, but they are also a contribution to that never-finished business, the *construction* of a socially-constituted self. Both of these processes invoke the earlier phases of the operation. Quite young children can be heard saying, 'when I was little...' To participate in conversation means among other things staying alert to autobiographic clues and traces, however oblique. Even the stereotype is a clumsy, but sometimes necessary, effort to do this. Thus the autobiographical impulse is a way of listening as well as a way of telling: it is essentially dialogic.

THE AUTOBIOGRAPHICAL IMPULSE IN INSTITUTIONAL DISCOURSE

Attentive examination of everyday discourse reveals that narrative surfaces easily and inevitably and without inhibition when the conversation is among intimates and no obvious and fateful judgments turn on the encounter (a job, jail, health, divorce). Oppressive power distorts and muffles it. de Certeau (1980: 41-2), in a remarkable paper, suggests that memory emerging as narrative is one means available to us for asserting our authority against institutionalized power, more precisely the discourses of power.

> Memory ....produces at the opportune moment a break which also inaugurates something new. It is the strangeness, the alien dynamic, of memory which gives it the power to transgress the law of the local space in question; from out of the unfathomable and ever-shifting secrets, there comes a sudden 'strike' ....details, intense singularities, which already function in memory as they do when circumstances give them an opportunity to intervene: the same timing in both occasions, the same artful relation between a concrete detail and a conjuncture, the latter figuring alternately as the trace of a past event, or as the production of some new harmony.

He goes on to link 'intense singularities' with story-telling. Scientific discourse, he says, exerts a careful maintenance over space which 'eliminates time's scandals.'

> Nonetheless, they return over and over again, noiselessly and surreptitiously, and not least within the scientific activity itself: not merely in the form of the practices of everyday life which go on even without their own discourse, but also in the sly and gossipy practices of everyday storytelling ....a practical know-how is at work in these stories, where all the features of the 'art of memory' itself can be detected ....the art of daily life can be witnessed in the tales told about it. (p. 42)

And, I would add, inevitably they are nearly always autobiographical.

To point this out does not necessarily mean that we must hasten to justify it by allocating the interest to some already established terrain and refer it, let us say, to the certain microfeatures of texts like deixis or cohesion (Halliday & Hasan 1976), or in a semiotic vein to explore the deep semantic structure of narrative (Greimas as discussed by Hawkes 1977), or in a narratological vein to look for signs of the implied or pseudonarrator. These are in themselves far from trivial enterprises. However you may know everything about the anatomy and physiology of a horse but that will tell you little or nothing about the horse as a commodity, or as a totem, or its obsolescence as a form of transport and beast of burden. My concern here lies in the periphery of the well-established discourses about narrative. The reason is simple. We need to understand, no matter how speculative and partial our efforts at this stage, the full significance of something which in our culture and in many (all?) others is a resource drawn on so heavily by everyone. Beyond that there is the need to understand why the autobiographical impulse is so constantly thwarted, put down, and often explicitly outlawed in our educational system and in 'high' discourse.

Ronald Fraser's (1984) autobiography uniquely combines his own recollections with the testimony, collected in interviews, of all those he knew in his childhood; it is thus a many-voiced work. All the voices speak of the same past. At the very end in a two-sided conversation he attempts to fix the impulse behind this exacting task:

- I've always thought history served one purpose at least. By discovering the major factors of change one can learn from them. The same ought to be true of an individual's history.

- Yes ....you want to be the subject of your history instead of the object you felt yourself to be . . .

- the subject, yes, but also the object. It's the synthesis of the two, isn't it.

- the author of your childhood then, the historian of

your past. (p.187)

To be the subject and object, both author and historian of one's own past, is asking a lot, but in this case justified by the book which precedes it. Come down the scale, or should I say across to another scale, to all those little anecdotes, recollections, episodes, and reminiscences which we all trade in, and we might say that a modest version of Fraser's aspiration asserts itself. Some can be the autobiographers of whole epochs of their lives and, using the written language, control It judiciously to keep subject and object always harmoniously in harness. But the impulse is the same whether we know it or not. Bakhtin (Volosinov 1976:87) says,

> In becoming aware of myself I attempt to look at myself through the eyes of another person ....Here we have the objective roots of even the most personal and intimate reactions.

I know of someone who wrote about her childhood, setting out to recount the games and inventive pastimes which seemed to her both inexhaustible and full of meaning. At the end of it she said thoughtfully, 'It's about a lonely childhood.' Thus in the art of articulating autobiography we do not simply unmask ourselves for others, we too await to know the face under the mask.

Genre

Once the autobiographical impulse makes enough space for itself, the tactics for which have been learned in many interactions, the archaeological practices of memory come under a minimum control of *genre* - the loose rules of which have been acquired through use, observation and the lessons of success and failure. The impulse is kept on a loose rein but a rein nonetheless. I am using the word genre in Bakhtin's sense. He proposes that speech genres are an essential part of language acquisition and have important consequences for thought.

> ....to learn to speak means to learn to construct utterances ....we learn to construct our speech in generic forms and when we hear the speech of others we deduce its genre from the first words; we anticipate in advance a certain volume ....as well as a certain compositional structure; we foresee the end; that is from the very beginning we have a sense of the speech whole. (Cited in Holquist 1983:314).

As utterance moves towards monologue, it is possible to perceive these genres much more clearly (a plan of action is proposed, a lay sermon delivered, such a one is denounced, a case is argued, etc.), though of course the monologue is always dialogic even when the other is silent. The autobiographical spoken narrative is so distinctive as to be swiftly recognized and identified. Bakhtin attributes to it certain features. For him (Medvedev/Bakhtin 1978:133) all speech genres constitute a way of thinking and learning.

> Every significant genre is a complex system of means and methods for the conscious control and finalization of reality.

and

> A particular aspect of reality can only be understood in connection with a particular means of representing it. (p. 134)

This is to take all those discussions about the relationship between thought and language on to a different plane and suggest that we think in the genres we have been furnished with through our experience of discourse. What Bakhtin calls 'the anecdote' requires the speaker to find and grasp the unity of an anecdotal event in life but it also 'presupposes an orientation towards the *means* for the development of narrative.'

> Every genre has its methods and means of seeing and conceptualising reality which are accessible to it alone. (p. 133)

These methods and means have been analyzed with great

finesse by structuralists like Genette (1980), Barthes (1982), and others but I am not aware of their having applied them to an autobiography or more particularly to autobiographical speech when the speaker already shares the past of his/her autobiography with those spoken to. These methods and means make the narrative of personal experience an essentially social activity. Such narratives are an interplay of concern for the material and a concern for the reception of it by others. But this is *not* to juxtapose the private and the public. The episodes of life past were already shaped by their social content and they are articulated in a socially constructed genre (i.e. methods and means socially created) and they are proffered as part of a social interchange.

However, these methods and means may well conceal from us, if we examine the text only, what is in the awareness of the participants and is shaping the narrative. Dunning (1985), working with oral narrative in her own classroom, elicited hospital stories from three of her students, aged fourteen. These stories do not arise from a sociolinguistic experiment. They were told in a regular story-telling session conducted with the whole class. Dunning is able to show how certain features of the story can be accounted for by the fact that all three story-tellers are negotiating their standing in the class.

David's standing at the time of his story-telling is fragile. He is back in school after a minor operation and, as Dunning says, 'suffering from the familiar re-entry pangs ....after an absence.' Thus in his story there are methods and means used to enable him to build up a tough, defiant, comic, slightly risqué character for himself and to suppress the anxiety he almost certainly felt at the time. This is an extract from David's story with the response of the listeners.

> D: I didn't go to sleep [the] last night. I was mucking around late. Nurse came in and 'it us 'cause we were mucking around in there.
> Pupil: Might've known.
> D: Night of the operation, we was reading comics Beano.... We 'ad the lights on and we 'eard the nurse say, 'Get that light out' and we didn't take no notice, just kept on reading. Then she came in next minute and hit us, just about, so I turned it out.
> Teacher: Hit us 'just about'. Did she hit you or just

threaten to hit you?
D: She said, 'Get into bed like this' (illustrates with a cuffing gesture) and I were just sitting there looking at 'er.
P: Yeah David.
P: Hard David.

David is receiving, and continues to receive beyond this point, the message from the class that his renegotiation of his standing is going quite well. This kind of narrative event is an interanimation of production and reception. The narrators, no longer invisible authors, have known or partly known motivations and aspirations. Here there is shared history. The personal narratives enter into a disclosure already begun which will continue beyond the ends of stories. In this respect written autobiographical discourse is quite different. It must enter the silent unknown.

Some while ago I began a written autobiographical narrative which would contrast sharply with an improvised narrative of the same events.

- Of course she thought of it. It wouldn't have crossed my mind.
- It would be nice, she said, a nice thing to do.
- Course, said my sister, you shouldn't get too big for your boots.
- You don't remember, said my mother, why should you remember? I remember.
- What'll I say to him? Remember me? The corner near the window, your favorite pupil. Turns out I am a genius. My mother thinks you ought to know. How's the little school going? Punishment Book filling up nicely?
- Such a clever-dick don't need a rehearsal, said my sister.
- Have a bit of heart, said my mother. You knock your kishkas out for twenty years teaching a bunch of snotty nosed momzeirim and in the finish what you got to show for it? Felling-hands, pressers, cutters, machinists, button-hole makers, market boys. Why shouldn't he know, now and then, that one of them won his matric?

- Passed, I said, not won, passed, together with thirty other future Nobel prize winners.
- Two a penny, said my sister. Pish, pish. It's a nothing.
- He'll go, he'll go, said my mother. A thank-you costs nothing.
- Did I say I wouldn't?
  My mother brushed the crumbs off the table into the palm of her hand and stood looking at them. She was so full of pride, she didn't know where to put it all.

Imagine a live telling of that story to the younger members of my family and you will know at once that the means and methods would have to be radically different. Nor, I hasten to add, would it be allowed to become a monologue. (I must leave it to you to work how it might go in different settings and why).

It must be clear that I am in certain respects privileging the autobiographical genre. If I do so, it is because some genres offer greater possibilities than others for certain purposes, are more dialogic, deploy a wider range of resources, are more open to individual working. The genre of parade ground language offers no play at all (though Yossarian had a try). In spontaneous conversation among intimates, self-imposed controls are at their lightest. In that setting the autobiographical impulse is likely to be strong and following it leaves the greatest room for manoeuvre; authorship asserts itself in everyone. Holquist (1983:314) puts it well.

> ....so that we may be understood, so that the work of the social world may continue, we must all, perforce, become authors. To use the shift of signs to represent the world is to use language for social relations ....Insofar as we wrest particular meanings out of general systems, we are all creators; a speaker is to his utterance what an author is to his text.

In the *now* of our speaking our efforts to find meaning in the world have as their richest resources the *then* of our past, perceived as events saturated with values and feelings. We do not, as we often say, relive the experience; we rework it to fashion it into a sense which we need to discover for its validity now and to share with others. We do not put on a rerun of the past; there is no switch we can throw and let the cameras run.

To tell of the past is to negotiate it, sometimes with love, sometimes with hate, but always with respect. The existence of a genre, learned in thousands of tellings, offers us a framework which promises order and control. I have only to begin, as I did very recently, like this:

My mother, who was always in a state of near paupery, always gave money to beggars in the street.

and I know that that sentence emerges from a long apprenticeship in the genre and that it is no sooner uttered than a set of choices beckons me which are all narrative choices, some of which will be so imperative that they might betray me into a loss of meaning or, as Derrida (1978: 4 - 6) puts it, to stifle the force under the form.

Authenticity

Labov (1972: 396) noted that oral accounts of personal experience command a unique attention from listeners.

Many of the narratives cited here rise to a very high level of competence; ....they will command the total attention of an audience in a remarkable way, certainly a deep and attentive silence that is never found in academic and political discussion.

But in spite of his interesting analysis he does not attempt to account for that 'deep and attentive silence.' I have been suggesting that the particular kind of attention we give arises because:

1. the power of narrative in general corresponds to a way of thinking and imagining;
2. it speaks with the voice of 'commonsense';
3. it invites us to consider not only the results of understanding but to live through the processes of reaching it;
4. it never tears asunder ideas and feelings; it moves us

by permitting us to enter the living space of another: it is perceived as testimony;
5. it specifically provides for the complicit engagement of the listener.

To try to put all this in one word I suggest *authenticity*. Let's explore this a little further.

Barthes (1982: 251) said that narrative is present at all times and in all places and that all human groups have their stories. So do individuals. But narrative is certainly not present in all places. In fact, there are places which are tacitly declared to be 'no-go' areas where, as Foucault (1970, 1977) suggests, both space and the discourse which belong with it are closely policed. Autobiographical stories often lie completely concealed beneath the genres which come to be defined precisely by their omission of personal stories. We are actually taught in the education system how to cover our narrative tracks and even to be ashamed of them.

Gilbert and Mulkay (1984), two sociologists, in a wicked book, tell us how they discovered that a very sharp controversy was going on in an area of biochemistry called oxidative phosphorylation. They go on to conduct research which would reveal how the dispute was played out, how scientists speak about such things. They interviewed those involved in Britain and the United States and examined the published papers. You can guess what emerged. In the interviews stories came tumbling out, like this one.

> He came running into the seminar, pulled me out with one of his other post-docs and took us to the back of the room and explained this idea that he had .... He was very excited. He was really high. He said, 'What if I told you that it didn't take any energy to make ATP at a catalytic site, it took energy to kick it off the catalytic site?' It took him about 30 seconds. But I was particularly predisposed to this idea. Everything I had been thinking, 12, 14, 16 different pieces of literature that could not be explained and then all of a sudden the simple explanation became clear .... And so we sat down and designed some experiments to prove, to test this.

> It took him about 30 seconds to sell it to me. It was really like a bolt. I felt, 'Oh my God, this must be right! Look at all the things it explains.'

The authors' comment reveals what happens to such stories in the academic culture:

> In the formal paper we are told that the experimental results suggested a model which seemed an improvement on previous assumptions and which was, accordingly, put to the test. In the interview we hear of a dramatic revelation of the central idea which was immediately seen to be right ....and which led to the design of new experiments.

Bakhtin would perhaps say, 'There you have the difference between *internally persuasive discourse* and *authoritative discourse.*' Standing behind them are two great forces always at work in language, the *centripetal* and the *centrifugal.* The centripetal is constituted from everything which pulls us towards a centre of linguistic norms at every level, the pressures to conform to one language, one dialect, one set of rules, the order of certain discourse etiquettes, and indeed genre conventions. The counter force is centrifugal which is constituted from everything which pulls away from the normative centre, the mixing of dialects, lexical and syntactical innovation, play with language, defiance of the genre conventions, use of a genre considered to be inappropriate, persistence of stigmatized language, phonological mockery. According to Bakhtin (1981: 272),

> Every concrete utterance of a speaking subject serves as a point where centrifugal as well as centripetal forces are brought to bear. The processes of centralization and decentralization, of unification and disunification, intersect in the utterance; .... it is in fact an active participant in such speech diversity.

There is no escaping centripetal forces; the question is what kind of discourse offers the greatest possibility to the play of centrifugal forces. For it must be clear that centripetal forces control or even suppress that crucial attempt which we all make to struggle against the given and already determined in language, a struggle which is an attempt to assert our own meanings against the matrix of ready-codified meanings lying in wait for us.

For Bakhtin the medium with most promise is the novel. I think there is a case for suggesting that autobiographical utterance is the folk novel. It is most impossible to police and springs up unpredictably outside the surveillance of the grammar book and the style manual. De Certeau (1980) argues that it is one of the means of outwitting established order, what he calls 'tactics.'

> Where dominating powers exploit the order of things, where ideological discourse represses or ignores, tactics fool this order and make it the field of their art. Thereby, the institution one is called to serve finds itself infiltrated by a style of social exchange, a style of technical invention, and a style of moral resistance - that is, by an economy of the 'gift' (generosities which are also ways of asking for something in return), by an aesthetic of 'moves', 'triumphs' or 'strikes' .... and by an ethic of tenacity .... This is what 'popular culture' really is and not some alien corpus, anatomised for the purposes of exhibit ....

Bakhtin saw the centrifugal in operation in parody, verbal masquerades, and in the folk buffoonery of local fairs. However the centrifugal can be attempted by anyone, the young included. In, for instance, Michael, aged 14, writing of his infant days:

> There was nothing.

> And I was two. Rabbit is my very best friend. I sat in a corner and we were playing with a thing and then there were reds and yellows and browns. My brother is Gonofan and he told Mummy (whose real name is also Mummy) to come and see the pretty colours. Mummy did not like them and hit the pretty colours.

> The deers in the park are brown. I like deers and I touched a deer and it ran away and I ran after it into the woods but she did not have a broomstick. She wanted

to eat me so I ran back to Mummy. I ran and ran like
Johnny Rabbit ran from the farmer's gun ....

I ran up the stairs with Rabbit. My bottom hurt and I
needed the potty. But I cannot run as fast as Rabbit and
I had to leave the brown gunge on the stairs and I wet
my eyes but I started to read and so was happy.

Mummy made me some red and blue shoes and
he played nic nac on my shoe
And I was three
He played nic nac on my knee

My Daddy (whose real name is also Daddy) is a good
wizard. He did magic on the house and made it change.
I went for a ride in the car and when I came back it had
changed but there was no room for Daddy in our new
house. He should have made it bigger

And I was four
He played nic nac on my door

I was with Rabbit on the pavement and we were
waiting for Daddy to make us be on holiday and a
young man, really the Giant up the beanstalk, made the
door sing like Penny Penguin. She says, 'Michael row
the boat ashore.' I was taken to be mended in hospital.

I think of all those who have laboured to discover the
essence of the 'well-formed story' and wonder what they would
make of that. The story eludes the centripetal tug by being
double-voiced; its surface texture is the voice of the infant from
two to four years (a changing voice in that time, you may have
noticed) but it is produced by a fourteen-year-old modernist
who knows how to manage the juxtaposition of images, abrupt
transitions, montage. The opening words defy centripetal
narrative, 'There was nothing.'

Deborah Tannen (1979) noted the widespread use of terms
in many disciplines to deal with patterns of expectations
(frames, scripts, schemata, scenes and so forth). There are two
ways in which this pattern of expectations can enter narrative
activity: (a) the recognition of an experience as a scene or

several scenes with narrative potential; (b) conforming to a pattern of expectations in the composition of actual narrative which tells the story of the scene. Now suppose we separate (a) and (b) by - a day, a month, twenty years. We now complicate the notion of frame enormously. Instead of a structure of expectation derived from past experience (i.e. a form of memory) and related to the presenting experience, we now have the intervention of memory in a different way. The *form* of presentation (narrative) fits the frame notion comfortably. But what does this telling filtered by memory and intervening experience do to the original experience? I suggest we now have a fascinating complexity - a new and bigger frame is placed around the original one which is at the same time definitely not discarded. It is this which constitutes the double-voice of autobiography. It is both how it was and how it is fused together. It may well account for the legitimate fictions of autobiography (perfectly 'remembered' conversations, for example). To sum up, a recognizable narrative is both constructed by and understood by a frame derived from past experience BUT the experience was originally understood by one frame and is now understood by a new one which includes understanding of the original frame.

Bakhtin was concerned to identify the essential differences between discourses which are, so to speak, compulsory and those which satisfy us by their feel of authenticity. He writes (1981:342) of 'two categories':

> .... in one, the authoritative word (religious, political, moral; the word of a father, of adults and of teachers, etc.) that does not know internal persuasiveness, in the other internally persuasive word that is denied all privilege, backed up by no authority at all, and is frequently not even acknowledged in society (not by public opinion, not by scholarly norms, nor by criticism) . . .

Authoritative discourse, he goes on to say, demands our unconditional allegiance - permits no play with its borders, no gradual and flexible transitions, no creative stylizing variants on it. It is indissolubly fused with its authority. It is all inertia and calcification, whereas

> Internally persuasive discourse .... is .... tightly interwoven with 'one's own word.' .... [It] is half-ours and half-someone else's .... [Its] semantic structure .... is not finite, it is open .... this discourse is able to reveal ever newer ways to mean. (pp. 345-46; italics in original)

Internally persuasive discourse is the arena in which autobiographical speech finds its scope and its diversity of intentions. Narratology has had a good run for its money but is not permitted to speak of such things (no authors, no intentions!). We must increasingly turn our attention to narrative as a form of participation in interaction when the narration is embedded in dialogue. We know that the story-teller can acquire or be offered the right to narrate, the chance to recruit the desires of the others, to achieve a moment's authority without being authoritative. We also have accumulating evidence that speakers can transform a turn in dialogue into a personal narrative which is a contribution to the goals of the dialogue; Erickson (1984) has shown how within a particular culture this is the prevailing mode and very disconcerting for those who do not share it. Halligan (1984) in studying over a long period the small group discussions of 12/13-year-old students in a black working-class inner-city area found a very similar pattern. In one analysis of a discussion (which turned on whether stealing is a result of poverty) he isolated five major personal anecdotes and demonstrated that,

> These anecdotes are the main structural members upon which the fabric of the discussion is erected, both because the discussion which intervenes is in reaction to them, and because they embody the logical structure of the discussion ....(p. 78)

You will not suppose that I am under the delusion that stories of personal experience will set the world to rights. I do, however, believe that from the top to the bottom of the educational system, authoritative discourse holds sway but that inroads into it can be made by giving students genuine fuller speaking rights in the classroom. An inevitable consequence will be the emergence of a much greater role for personal narrative. For most students this would constitute a liberation. In the end stories about the past are also about the future. On the other hand, we have only to remind ourselves of the way in which folk story was domesticated into cosiness, to remember that stories themselves can kow-tow with subservience. Their very universality contains its own surreptitious menace. They can be used to manipulate, control, create a market, and above all to massage us into forgetfulness and passivity. Nor do I wish to forget that alongside the autobiographical impulse there is the autobiographical *compulse* of the courtroom, of the government inspector, of the attitude tests, of the curriculum vitae, of the torture chamber. There are some very sinister people engaged in hermeneutics! We are not left free to limit our pasts to unpoliced crannies and congenial moments. Stand and deliver. There are many ways in which power attempts to wrest from us our past and use it for its own ends. Our autobiographies also figure in dossiers wrung from us as surely as were confessions by the Inquisition. Such invitations do not coax and tempt memory for they surround it with caution, fear, and even terror.

Yet in spite of the inquisitors, indeed, in stark defiance of them, we have no alternative. We must persist with archaeological expeditions into the substrata of our memories so that, returning, we may look the present in the eye and even dare to peer into the future.

Footnotes

1. The three volumes consisted of Hymes (1973) plus a new foreword and postscript written in 1982; all three have been published in French (Hymes 1984) but not in English.

2. Dell Hymes's awareness of these issues is put powerfully and delicately in a joint paper (Hymes and Cazden, 1980:130):
'In sum, our cultural stereotypes predispose us to dichotomize forms and functions of language use ....And one side of the dichotomy tends to be identified with cognitive superiority. In point of fact, however, none of the usual elements of conventional dichotomies are certain guides to level of cognitive activity. In particular, narrative may be a complementary, or alternative mode of thinking.'
Just to leave us in no doubt, he concludes with what he calls *Warm Springs Interlude,* rich with his own autobiographical narrative and observations of narrative in the lives of the Indian people he knows: '- It is the grounding of performance and text

in a narrative view of life. That is to say, a view of life as a potential source of narrative. Incidents, even apparently slight incidents, have pervasively the potentiality of an interest that is worth retelling .... A certain potentiality, of shared narrative form, on the one hand, of consequentiality, on the other.' (p. 135)

References

Bakhtin, M.M. (1981), *The Dialogic Imagination*, ed. by Michael Holquist, trans. by Caryl Emerson & Michael Holquist. Austin: University of Texas Press.
Barthes, Roland (1982), 'Introduction to the Structural Analysis of Narrative',
Barthes: Selected writings, ed. by Susan Sontag, 251-95. London: Fontana.
de Certeau, Michel (1980), *On the Oppositional Practices of Everyday Life*. Social Text 1:3.3~3.
Chambers, Ross (1984), *Story and Situation*. Minneapolis: University of Minnesota Press.
Derrida, Jacques (1978), *Writing and Difference*, trans. by A. Bass. London: Routledge & Kegan Paul.
Dunning, Jean (1985), Reluctant and Willing Story-tellers in the Classroom. *English in Education* 19.1-1.15.
Eco, Umberto (1983), *The Name of the Rose*. San Diego: Harcourt Brace Jovanovich.
Erickson, Fredrick (1984), 'Rhetoric, Anecdote, and Rhapsody: Coherence Strategies in a Conversation among Black American Adolescents' *Coherence in Spoken and Written Discourse*, ed. by Deborah Tannen, 81-154. Norwood, NJ: Ablex.
Fraser, Ronald (1984), *In search of a Past*. London: Verso.
Foucault, Michel (1970), *The Order of Things: An Archaeology of the Human Sciences*. London: Tavistock.
Foucault, Michel (1977), *Discipline and Punish: The Birth of the Prison*. New York: Pantheon.
Genette, Gerard (1980), *Narrative Discourse*, trans. by Jane E. Lewin. London: Basil Blackwell.
Gilbert, G. Nigel and Mulkay, Michael (1984), *Opening Pandora's Box*. Cambridge: University Press.
Halliday, M.A.K, and Ruqaiya Hasan (1976), *Cohesion in English*. London: Longman.
Halligan, David (1984), *Social Context, Discourse, and Learning*

in Small Group Discussion. PhD dissertation, University of London.

Hawkes, Terence (1977), *Structuralism and Semiotics*. London: Methuen.

Holquist, Michael (1983), Answering as Authoring: Mikhail Bakhtin's Translinguistics. *Critical Inquiry* 10:2.307-19.

Hymes, Dell (1973), 'Toward Linguistic Competence', *Texas Working Papers in Sociolinguistics* No. 16. Austin, TX: Southwest Educational Development Laboratory.

Hymes, Dell (1984), *Vers la Competence de Communication*, trans. by Frances Mugler, with 'Note liminaire' by Daniel Coste. Langues et Apprentissage des Langues; Collection Dirigee par H. Besse et E. Papo, Ecole Normale Superieure de Saint-Cloud. Paris: Hatier-Credif

Hymes, Dell and Cazden, Courtney. (1980), 'Narrative Thinking and Storytelling Rights: A Folklorist's Clue to a Critique of Education'. *Language in Education: Ethnolinguistic Essays*, ed. by Dell Hymes, 126-38. Washington, DC: Center for Applied Linguistics.

Labov, William (1972), *Language in the Inner City*. Philadelphia: University of Pennsylvania Press.

Medvedev, P.N./M.M. Bakhtin (1978), *The Formal Method in Literary Scholarship: A Critical Introduction to Sociological Poetics*. Baltimore: Johns Hopkins University Press.

Tannen, Deborah (1979), 'What's in a Frame? Surface Evidence for Underlying Expectations'. *New Directions in Discourse Processing*, ed. by Roy O. Freedle, 137-81. Norwood, NJ: Ablex.

Volosinov, V.N. [M.M. Bakhtin] (1976), *Freudianism: A Marxist Critique*, trans. by I.R. Titunik New York: Academic.